Math in Focus®
Singapore Math®
by Marshall Cavendish

Extra Practice

Author
Bernice Lau Pui Wah

Marshall Cavendish
Education

U.S. Distributor

Houghton
Mifflin
Harcourt

COMMON CORE

© Copyright 2009, 2013 Edition Marshall Cavendish International (Singapore) Private Limited
© 2014 Marshall Cavendish Education Pte Ltd

Published by Marshall Cavendish Education
Times Centre, 1 New Industrial Road, Singapore 536196
Customer Service Hotline: (65) 6213 9444
US Office Tel: (1-914) 332 8888 | Fax: (1-914) 332 8882
E-mail: tmesales@mceducation.com
Website: www.mceducation.com

Distributed by
Houghton Mifflin Harcourt
222 Berkeley Street
Boston, MA 02116
Tel: 617-351-5000
Website: www.hmheducation.com/mathinfocus

First published 2009
2013 Edition

Math in Focus® Extra Practice 4A
ISBN 978-0-669-01591-1

Printed in Singapore

6 7 8   1401   18 17 16 15
4500557951   A B C D E

Contents

Introducing

Math in Focus®

Extra Practice

Extra Practice 4A and *4B*, written to complement *Math in Focus®: Singapore Math®* by Marshall Cavendish Grade 4, offer further practice very similar to the Practice exercises in the Student Books and Workbooks for on-level students.

Extra Practice provides ample questions to reinforce all the concepts taught, and includes challenging questions in the Put on Your Thinking Cap! pages. These pages provide extra non-routine problem-solving opportunities, strengthening critical thinking skills.

Extra Practice is an excellent option for homework, or may be used in class or after school. It is intended for students who simply need more practice to become confident, or secure students who are aiming for excellence.

BLANK

Write the missing words and digits for each number.

17.   thirty-eight thousand, _____   3____,050

18.   forty-one _____, two hundred ten   41,____10

19.   seventy-five thousand, _____ hundred six   75,30____

20.   ninety-nine thousand, _____-four   99,____44

Make each 5-digit number using all the cards. Do not begin a number with '0'.

21.   A number with 6 in the thousands place: _____

22.   A number with 3 in the ten thousands place and

8 in the tens place: _____

23.   The least possible number: _____

24.   The greatest possible number: _____

25.   The least possible even number: _____

26.   The greatest possible odd number: _____

Make each 5-digit number using all the cards.
Do not begin a number with '0'.

27. The least possible number with 2 in the tens place: _____

28. The greatest possible number with 9 in the ones place: _____

29. The least possible odd number: _____

30. The least possible even number: _____

31. The greatest possible odd number: _____

32. The greatest possible even number: _____

Lesson 1.1   Numbers to 100,000 (Part 2)

Complete.

In 52,896,

1.   the digit 2 is in the _____ place.

2.   the digit 6 is in the _____ place.

3.   the digit 5 is in the _____ place.

4.   the digit 9 is in the _____ place.

5.   the digit 8 is in the _____ place.

In 91,485,

6.   the value of the digit 4 is _____.

7.   the value of the digit 5 is _____.

8.   the value of the digit 9 is _____.

9.   the value of the digit 8 is _____.

10.   the value of the digit 1 is _____.

Write the missing numbers and words.

In 73,824,

11. the digit 4 stands for _____ ones.

12. the value of the digit 2 is _____.

13. the digit in the ten thousands place is _____.

14. the digit 8 stands for _____ hundreds.

15. the digit 3 is in the _____ place.

In 96,743,

16. the digit 4 is in the _____ place.

17. the digit 9 stands for _____.

18. the digit 3 is in the _____ place.

19. the value of the digit 6 is _____.

20. the digit _____ is in the hundreds place and

its value is _____.

Fill in the blanks.

21.   23,485 = 2 ten thousands + _____ thousands +

_____ hundreds + 8 tens + 5 ones

22.   72,586 = _____ ten thousands + 2 thousands +

5 hundreds + _____ tens + _____ ones

23.   20,000 + 4,000 + 700 + 8 = 2 _____ + 4 _____ +

7 _____ + _____ ones

24.   90,000 + 800 + 50 = _____ + _____ + 5 _____

Write each number in expanded form by completing the number sentence.

25.   24,329 = _____ + 4,000 + _____ + _____ + 9

26.   37,486 = 30,000 + _____ + 400 + _____ + 6

27.   42,635 = 40,000 + _____ + _____ + _____ + 5

28.   56,666 = _____ + _____ + 600 + _____ + 6

29.   99,854 = _____ + _____ + _____ +

_____ + 4

Solve. Use the place-value charts to help you.

30. Find the mystery number using these clues.
- It is a 5-digit even number.
- The digit 3 is in the hundreds place.
- The value of the digit 4 is 40.
- The digit 6 stands for 6 ones.
- The digit in the ten thousands place is twice the digit in the tens place.
- The value of the digit in the thousands place is 30 times the value of the digit in the hundreds place.

Ten Thousands	Thousands	Hundreds	Tens	Ones

The number is _____.

31. Find the mystery number using these clues.
- It is a 4-digit odd number.
- All the digits are different.
- None of the digits are 0 or 9.
- The tens digit is twice the ones digit, and the hundreds digit is twice the tens digit.
- The thousands digit is one less than the hundreds digit.

Thousands	Hundreds	Tens	Ones

The number is _____.

Lesson 1.2   Comparing Numbers to 100,000

Write > or < in each ◯.

1. 78,309 ◯ 78,093   **2.** 39,807 ◯ 39,870

3. 87,930 ◯ 89,730   **4.** 98,730 ◯ 98,073

Compare these numbers.

| 26,653 | 60,002 | 91,111 | 80,888 |

5. Write the least number. _____

6. Write the greatest number. _____

7. Write the greatest odd number. _____

8. Write the least even number. _____

Order these numbers.

9. Begin with the least:

_____

10. Begin with the greatest:

_____

61,352   61,253   61,532

76,138   78,631   78,061

Fill in the blanks.

11.   5,000 less than 81,250 is _____.

12.   30,000 more than 48,900 is _____.

13.   20,000 more than 36,500 is _____.

14.   _____ is 8,000 less than 53,990.

15.   _____ is 6,500 less than 38,620.

16.   49,500 is 6,000 more than _____.

17.   13,800 is 9,000 less than _____.

18.   46,500 is 15,500 less than _____.

Continue the number patterns.
Then write the rule for each pattern.

19.   30,480   30,680   30,880   _____   _____

       Rule: _____

20.   54,200   55,700   57,200   _____   _____

       Rule: _____

21.   63,120   63,720   64,120   64,720   _____   _____

       Rule: _____

22.   18,250   18,500   19,000   20,000   _____   _____

       Rule: _____

Name: _____   **Date:** _____

 **Put on Your Thinking Cap!**

A 5-digit number has five different even digits.

1.   What is the greatest possible number these 5 digits

can form? _____

Use the number in Exercise 1 to answer the following.

2.   What is the value of the digit in the hundreds place? _____

3.   What is the value of the digit in the ten thousands place? _____

Continue the patterns.

4.   1 12 23 34 _____ _____

5.   256 225 196 169 _____ _____

6.   2 8 18 32 50 _____ _____ _____

7.   3,650 3,850 4,250 5,050 _____ _____

8.   4,400 4,550 4,850 5,300 _____ _____

Name: _____ **Date:** _____

Fill in the blanks.

9. The least possible 4-digit number is _____.

10. The greatest possible 4-digit number is _____.

11. The least possible 4-digit odd number is _____.

12. The greatest possible 4-digit odd number is _____.

13. The least possible 4-digit even number is _____.

14. The greatest possible 4-digit even number is _____.

15. The least possible 4-digit number that has 3 as one

of its digits is _____.

16. The greatest possible 4-digit number that has 5 as one

of its digits is _____.

17. The least possible 4-digit number that has 0 as one digit,

and in which no digit is repeated is _____.

18. The greatest possible 4-digit number that has 0 as one digit,

and in which no digit is repeated is _____.

© Marshall Cavendish International (Singapore) Private Limited.

2 Estimation and Number Theory

Lesson 2.1   Estimation

Find each sum or difference. Then use rounding or front-end estimation to check that your answers are reasonable.

1.   649 + 385 = _____

   Estimated sum: _____

2.   2,264 + 8,721 = _____

   Estimated sum: _____

3.   538 − 269 = _____

   Estimated difference: _____

4.   18,460 − 485 = _____

   Estimated difference: _____

Find each product. Then use rounding or front-end estimation to check that your answers are reasonable.

5.   282 × 3 = _____

   Estimated product: _____

6.   119 × 5 = _____

   Estimated product: _____

7.   188 × 4 = _____

   Estimated product: _____

Find each quotient. Then use related multiplication facts to check that your answers are reasonable.

8.   76 ÷ 4 = _____   Estimated quotient: _____

9.   98 ÷ 2 = _____   Estimated quotient: _____

10. 87 ÷ 3 = _____   Estimated quotient: _____

Solve. Decide whether to find an estimate or an exact answer.

11.   Mr. Jackson has $8,000. He wants to buy the following items.

microwave   toaster   oven   coffee machine

Complete the table.

Item	Actual Cost	Rounded to the Nearest Hundred
microwave	$_____	$_____
toaster	$_____	$_____
oven	$_____	$_____
coffee machine	$_____	$_____

Does Mr. Jackson have enough money to pay for all the items? _____

Lesson 2.2   Factors

Answer each question. Write *Yes* or *No*.

1. Is 6 a factor of 72? _____
2. Is 8 a factor of 84? _____

3. Is 7 a factor of 98? _____
4. Is 4 a factor of 98? _____

5. Is 9 a factor of 108? _____
6. Is 5 a factor of 125? _____

7. Is 7 a factor of 86? _____
8. Is 6 a factor of 96? _____

**Find the common factors of each number pair.
Then find the greatest factor.**

36	60

9. The factors of 36 are _____.

10. The factors of 60 are _____.

11. The common factors of 36 and 60 are _____.

12. The greatest common factor of 36 and 60 is _____.

84	72

13. The factors of 84 are _____.

14. The factors of 72 are _____.

15. The common factors of 84 and 72 are _____.

16. The greatest common factor of 84 and 72 is _____.

Look at the numbers. Fill in the blanks.

24   30   45   27   18   50

17. Write all the numbers that have 3 as a factor. _____

18. Write all the numbers that have 6 as a factor. _____

19. Write all the numbers that have 3 and 6 as factors. _____

Complete. Find the prime and composite numbers.

9   15   19   26   33   37   45   47

20. The prime numbers are _____.

21. The composite numbers are _____.

Find the prime and composite numbers in each set.

22. Write the next six prime numbers after 10.

_____

23. Write all the composite numbers between 20 and 30.

_____

Lesson 2.3   Multiples

Fill in the blanks.

1.   The fifth multiple of 8 is _____.

2.   The eighth multiple of 9 is _____.

3.   The twelfth multiple of 6 is _____.

4.   The eleventh multiple of 7 is _____.

5.   The seventh multiple of 10 is _____.

Find the common multiples of each pair of numbers.
Then find the least common multiple.

4 and 9

6.   The first 18 multiples of 4 are _____

_____.

7.   The first 8 multiples of 9 are _____.

8.   The first two common multiples of 4 and 9 are _____.

9.   The least common multiple of 4 and 9 is _____.

6 and 8

10.   The first 8 multiples of 6 are _____.

11.   The first 8 multiples of 8 are _____.

12.   The first two common multiples of 6 and 8 are _____.

13.   The least common multiple of 6 and 8 is _____.

Find the least common multiple of each pair of numbers.

14. 7 and 8   **15.** 9 and 12

16. 10 and 12   **17.** 15 and 20

Use these numbers to fill in the blanks.

54   20   48   60   72

18. Write all the numbers that are multiples of 4.

_____

19. Write all the numbers that are multiples of 8.

_____

20. Write all the numbers that are multiples of 9.

_____

21. Find the number that is the least common multiple of 4, 8, and 9.

_____

 Put on Your Thinking Cap!

Solve.

1. A number is between 10 and 20.
It is also a factor of 24. What is the number?

2. It is a 3-digit number.
All the digits are different.
The first and second digits are multiples of 3.
The first digit is greater than the second digit.

The sum of the first two digits is 7 more than the third digit.
The number is not a multiple of 5.
The third digit is greater than 3.

What is the number? _____

3. Jane's age is a two-digit multiple of 4. Next year, her age will be
a multiple of 5. How old is Jane now?

© Marshall Cavendish International (Singapore) Private Limited.

Solve.

4.   Mrs. Garcia watches 16 students cycle home after school. She counts 38 wheels. Some of the students are on bicycles, and the rest are on tricycles. How many students are on bicycles?

5.   Michelle has less than 50 baseball cards. If she puts them in packs of 7, she has 5 baseball cards left. If she puts them in packs of 9, she has 6 baseball cards left. How many baseball cards does Michelle have?

6. Susan's birthday is in January.
- The date has two digits.
- You say the date when you count by fours.
- The date is divisible by 6.
- The sum of the digits is 3.

When is Susan's birthday? _____

7. Nathan's birthday is also in January.
- The date has two digits.
- The date can only be divided by 1 and by itself.
- The sum of the digits is 8.

When is Nathan's birthday? _____

8.   Daniel has won $20 worth of prizes. He can choose from these prizes.

Show the ways in which he can select $20 worth of prizes. Use ✔ to show the number of each prize he can choose.

Adventure Books ($4)	Soft Toys ($6)	Games ($8)

CHAPTER 3 Whole Number Multiplication and Division

Lesson 3.1   Multiplying by a 1-Digit Number

Multiply 2,658 by 7 and find the missing numbers.

1. | Step 1 | 8 ones × 7 = _____ ones

= _____ tens _____ ones

2. | Step 2 | _____ tens × 7 = _____ tens

= _____ hundreds _____ tens

3. | Step 3 | _____ hundreds × 7 = _____ hundreds

= _____ thousands _____ hundreds

4. | Step 4 | _____ thousands × 7 = _____ thousands

= _____ ten thousand _____ thousands

5.

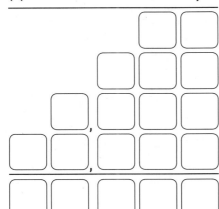

Find each product.

6.
```
      4   9   5
  ×           8
  ⬚,⬚⬚⬚
```

7.
```
      8   9   8
  ×           4
  ⬚,⬚⬚⬚
```

8.
```
      9   2   7
  ×           9
  ⬚,⬚⬚⬚
```

9.
```
      9   9   3
  ×           5
  ⬚,⬚⬚⬚
```

10.
```
   3,  5   8   9
  ×           3
  ⬚⬚,⬚⬚⬚
```

11.
```
   2,  6   7   8
  ×           6
  ⬚⬚,⬚⬚⬚
```

12.
```
   7,  2   3   1
  ×           3
  ⬚⬚,⬚⬚⬚
```

13.
```
   4,  9   6   3
  ×           7
  ⬚⬚,⬚⬚⬚
```

14.
```
   5,  4   9   7
  ×           8
  ⬚⬚,⬚⬚⬚
```

15.
```
   4,  8   3   6
  ×           7
  ⬚⬚,⬚⬚⬚
```

© Marshall Cavendish International (Singapore) Private Limited.

Lesson 3.2 Multiplying by a 2-Digit Number

Write the missing numbers.

1. 48 × 10 = _____	**2.** 89 × 10 = _____
3. 23 × 40 = 23 × _____ tens = _____ tens = _____	**4.** 35 × 30 = 35 × _____ tens = _____ tens = _____
5. 419 × 50 = 419 × _____ tens = _____ tens = _____	**6.** 627 × 20 = 627 × _____ tens = _____ tens = _____
7. 536 × 60 = 536 × ____ × 10 = _____ × 10 = _____	**8.** 648 × 60 = 648 × ____ × 10 = _____ × 10 = _____

Find each product.

9. $87 \times 7 =$ _____ $87 \times 70 =$ _____	**10.** $96 \times 7 =$ _____ $96 \times 70 =$ _____
11. $356 \times 8 =$ _____ $356 \times 80 =$ _____	**12.** $267 \times 9 =$ _____ $267 \times 90 =$ _____

Estimate each product.

> *Example*
>
> 52×23 is about <u>50</u> $\times$ <u>20</u>.
> Estimate: <u>50 $\times$ 20 = 1,000</u>

13. 87×39 is about _____ $\times$ _____.

        Estimate: _____

14. 369×47 is about _____ $\times$ _____.

        Estimate: _____

● **Multiply. Then estimate to check that your answers are reasonable.**

15.   9   8
        ×   7   6
      ―――――――――

16.   5   4
        ×   9   7
      ―――――――――

17.   3   6   4
        ×   2   9
      ―――――――――――

18.   5   2   8
        ×   4   6
      ―――――――――――

Name: _____ **Date:** _____

Multiply. Then estimate to check that your answers are reasonable.

19.
```
      3   9   2
  ×       3   0
  _____
```

20.
```
      4   3   9
  ×       7   2
  _____
```

21.
```
      7   3   4
  ×       8   6
  _____
```

22.
```
      8   5   6
  ×       9   4
  _____
```

Lesson 3.3   Modeling Division with Regrouping

Complete the steps.

1.

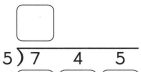

5)7 4 5

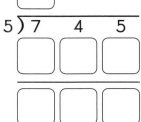

2.

6)9 8 4

Divide.

3. $2\overline{)7\quad2\quad8}$

4. $3\overline{)7\quad3\quad5}$

5. $4\overline{)9\quad4\quad8}$

6. $5\overline{)9\quad3\quad0}$

7. $6\overline{)6\quad5\quad4}$

8. $7\overline{)9\quad7\quad3}$

9. $8\overline{)9\quad8\quad4}$

10. $9\overline{)9\quad5\quad4}$

Lesson 3.4   Dividing by a 1-Digit Number

Fill in the blanks to find each quotient.

1. $6,400 \div 8 =$ _____ hundreds $\div 8$

   $=$ _____ hundreds

   $=$ _____

2. $6,300 \div 9 =$ _____ hundreds $\div 9$

   $=$ _____ hundreds

   $=$ _____

3. $9,000 \div 3 =$ _____ thousands $\div 3$

   $=$ _____ thousands

   $=$ _____

Estimate each quotient.

4. $78 \div 4$ is about _____ $\div 4$.   Estimate: _____

5. $397 \div 5$ is about _____ $\div 5$.   Estimate: _____

6. $7,425 \div 5$ is about _____ $\div 5$.   Estimate: _____

7. $6,726 \div 6$ is about _____ $\div 6$.   Estimate: _____

Divide.

8. $4\overline{)5,\ \ 0\ \ \ 5\ \ \ 2}$ **9.** $6\overline{)6,\ \ 0\ \ \ 7\ \ \ 8}$

10. $7\overline{)1,\ \ 9\ \ \ 8\ \ \ 8}$ **11.** $9\overline{)5,\ \ 0\ \ \ 5\ \ \ 8}$

12. $8\overline{)3,\ \ 9\ \ \ 7\ \ \ 6}$ **13.** $5\overline{)4,\ \ 8\ \ \ 4\ \ \ 0}$

Find each quotient. Then estimate to check that your answers are reasonable.

14. $1,748 \div 7 =$ _____ R _____

15. $3,871 \div 4 =$ _____ R _____

16. $3,014 \div 8 =$ _____ R _____

17. $2,518 \div 9 =$ _____ R _____

Find each quotient. Then estimate to check that your answers are reasonable.

18. $5{,}453 \div 9 =$ _____ R _____

19. $7{,}218 \div 8 =$ _____ R _____

20. $6{,}499 \div 7 =$ _____ R _____

21. $2{,}781 \div 5 =$ _____ R _____

Lesson 3.5   Real-World Problems: Multiplication and Division

1.   A digital camera costs $699. A retailer sells 38 cameras. How much does he collect altogether?

2.   A bakery sells 369 banana muffins each day. It sells 4 times as many blueberry muffins as banana muffins each day. How many blueberry muffins are sold every day?

3. A factory produces 1,899 toy cars each day. How many toy cars does it produce in 7 days?

4. Ms. Marquez divides 3,438 beads equally among 6 groups of students for a crafts project. How many beads does each group have?

5. 2,255 stamps are divided equally among 6 post offices.
   a. How many stamps does each post office receive?

   b. How many stamps are left over?

6. Each pair of in-line skates costs $56.
   a. How much does a store have to pay for 39 pairs of in-line skates?

   b. A store sells each pair of in-line skates for $72. What is the profit that the store makes on the 39 pairs of in-line skates?

7. Hannah gave $68 to charity. Hannah's mother gave 25 times as much as Hannah. How much did they give altogether?

8. A fruit seller has 2,400 oranges. He throws away 15 rotten oranges and packs the remainder equally into 9 boxes. How many oranges are in each box?

9. There are 4 times as many children as adults at a theater.
There are 475 adults. How many people are at the theater altogether?

10. A nature club has 37 members. Each member receives 15 fish to put
into an aquarium. If 20 of the total number of fish are put into a fishbowl
instead, how many fish are put into the aquarium?

© Marshall Cavendish International (Singapore) Private Limited.

11. Mr. Joseph's salary is $3,650. He spends $1,610 on rent. He divides the rest of his salary into 3 parts for his other monthly expenses. How much money is in each part?

12. Diana mixes 1,543 milliliters of orange concentrate with 932 milliliters of water to make orange juice. She then pours the mixture equally into 9 glasses. How much orange juice is in each glass?

Put on Your Thinking Cap!

1.   Sarah has 275 red beads and 3 times as many blue beads. She uses a total of 156 beads to make a bracelet. How many beads are left?

2.   Factory A produces 420 footballs a day. Factory B produces 90 fewer footballs than Factory A each day. How many footballs do the two factories produce in 28 days?

3.   James and Sam saved $392 altogether. Sam had 3 times as much money as James. Sam spends $38 on a pair of shoes. How much money does Sam have now?

4.   Mr. Roberts inherits some money. He keeps $1,800 for himself, gives $980 to his wife, and divides the rest among his 6 children. Each of his children receives $89. How much did Mr. Roberts inherit?

5.   Mrs. Rodin buys a table and 6 chairs for $1,233. The table costs $750 more than each chair. How much does Mrs. Rodin pay for the 6 chairs?

6.   Ms. Rao buys a computer, a printer, and a scanner for $2,543. The computer costs $1,502 more than the printer. The printer costs $123 more than the scanner. How much does Ms. Rao pay for the computer?

7. Use each of the digits 2, 4, 7, 8, and 9 only once.
Arrange the digits in these boxes to get

a. the greatest possible product.

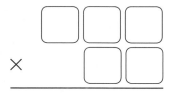

b. the least possible product.

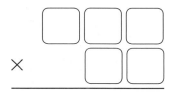

8. Mr. Garcia's age this year is a multiple of 7. In 3 years, his age will be
a multiple of 5. He is more than 20 years but less than 80 years old.
How old will Mr. Garcia be in 6 years?

9. At a bicycle shop, a bicycle costs $49 and a tricycle costs $27.
An after-school club buys bicycles and tricycles with a total of 39 wheels.
The club buys 2 more bicycles than tricycles.
a. How many bicycles does the club buy?

b. How much money does the club pay for the bicycles?

CHAPTER 4 Tables and Line Graphs

Lesson 4.1   Making and Interpreting a Table

Use the data to complete the table.

Evergreen School held a competition to choose the top junior sports player of the year. The records of the top four female players are listed below.

Name: Maria
Basketball points: 88
Baseball runs: 59

Name: Jade
Basketball points: 110
Baseball runs: 64

Name: Judith
Basketball points: 121
Baseball runs: 60

Name: Stacy
Basketball points: 88
Baseball runs: 57

1.   **Top Female Junior Sports Players**

Name	Basketball Points	Baseball Runs
Maria		
Jade		
Judith		
Stacy		

Use the data from the table to complete each sentence.

2.   _____ scored the greatest number of baseball runs.

      She scored _____ runs.

3.   _____ and _____ scored the same number of basketball points.

4.   Jade scored _____ more baseball runs than Stacy.

Adrian counted the number of living things in his garden.

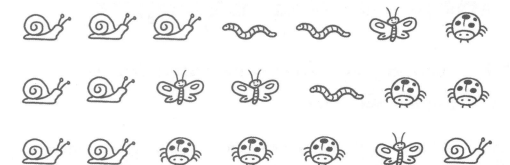

Make tally marks to count the number of each type of living thing.

5.   **Living Things**

Snails	
Worms	
Ladybugs	
Butterflies	

Use the data in the tally chart to complete the table.

6.   **Number of Living Things**

Snails	
Worms	
Ladybugs	
Butterflies	

Use the data from the table to complete each sentence.

7.   There are _____ worms.

8.   There are _____ ladybugs and butterflies altogether.

9.   There are 9 _____ and _____ altogether.

10.   There are twice as many _____ as _____.

● The bar graph shows the different types of bread loaves sold at a bakery in a week.

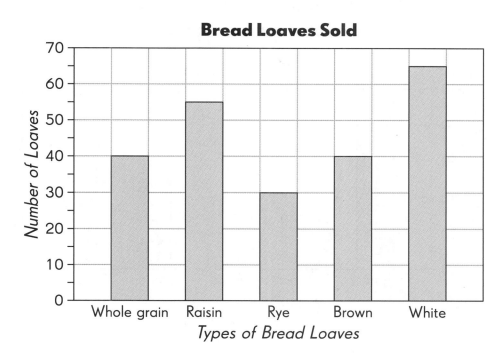

Bread Loaves Sold

● **Use the data in the graph to complete the table. Then use the data to complete the sentences.**

11.   **Bread Loaves Sold**

Whole grain bread	
Raisin bread	
Rye bread	
Brown bread	
White bread	

12. The greatest number of bread loaves sold was _____.

13. An equal number of _____ bread loaves and

_____ bread loaves were sold.

14. 25 more loaves of _____ bread were sold than

_____ bread or _____ bread.

Use the bar graph to answer the questions.

The bar graph shows the favorite books of a group of students.

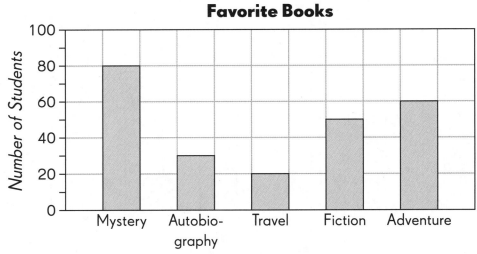

15. Which type of book did the most students like? _____

16. Which type of book did the fewest students like?

_____

17. How many students were surveyed? _____

18. How many students liked adventure books and mystery books

altogether? _____

19. How many students liked travel books and autobiography books

altogether? _____

20. How many more students liked mystery books than travel

books? _____

Lesson 4.2   Using a Table

Use the data in the table to complete the sentences.

The table shows different fruits at rows, columns, and intersections.

	Column 1	Column 2	Column 3	Column 4	Column 5
Row A	🍎			🍓	
Row B		🍊			🍐
Row C			🍒		
Row D	🍇		🍑		
Row E					🍋

1. (pear) is at the intersection of Row _____ and Column _____.

2. (lemon) is at the intersection of Row _____ and Column _____.

3. (strawberry) is in Row _____ and Column _____.

4. (grapes) is in Row _____ and Column _____.

5. Shade the intersection of Row E and Column 2.

Name: _____ **Date:** _____

Complete the table. Then answer the questions.

Students from four grades play sports after school — soccer, badminton, baseball, and basketball. The number of students who play each sport is shown in the table below.

Sports Played by Students

Grade	Soccer	Badminton	Baseball	Basketball
2	6	10		12
3	6	9	8	
4		7	14	10
5	7		6	11
Total	28	42	40	50

6. Which is the most popular sport? _____

7. Which is the least popular sport? _____

8. How many more students in the third grade play basketball than

in the fifth grade? _____

9. How many students play badminton altogether? _____

10. How many more students play basketball than badminton

altogether? _____

11. Which grade has twice as many students playing baseball

as the fifth grade? _____

12. How many fewer students play soccer than baseball? _____

Name: _____   **Date:** _____

Lesson 4.3 Line Graphs

Use the data in the line graphs to answer each question.

The line graph below shows the change in Taylor's savings over 6 months.

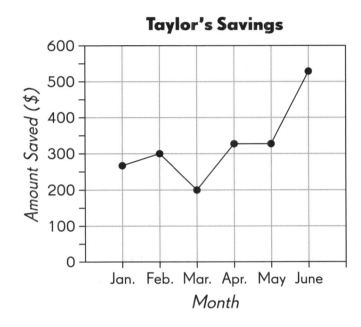

1. In which month did Taylor have the greatest amount in her savings?

   _____

2. In which month did she have the least amount in her savings?

   _____

3. In which months did she have the same amount saved?

   _____ and _____

4. Did Taylor's savings between January and June increase

   or decrease? _____

The line graph shows the number of falafels Mr. Clarkson had in his bakery at different times of the day.

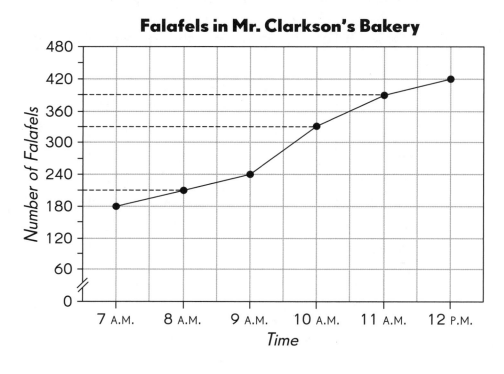

Falafels in Mr. Clarkson's Bakery

5. At what time did Mr. Clarkson have 240 falafels in his bakery? _____

6. At what time was the number of falafels twice as much as

at 8 A.M.? _____

7. During which 2-hour interval was the increase in the number of falafels the greatest? How much was the increase?

_____

_____

The line graph shows the temperature at different times in New York one morning.

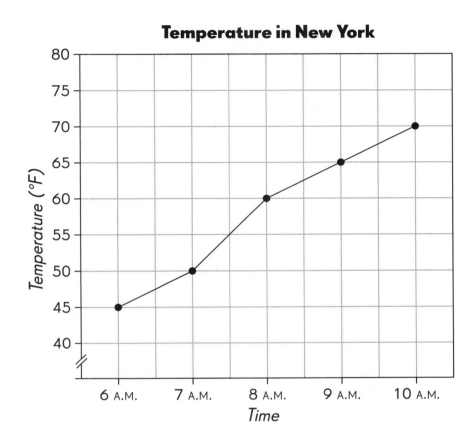

Temperature in New York

8. What was the temperature at 7 A.M.? _____°F

9. What was the temperature at 9 A.M.? _____°F

10. During which 1-hour interval was the increase in temperature

    the greatest? _____

11. How many hours did it take for the temperature to rise

    from 45°F to 65°F? _____

The line graph shows the change in the number of flu patients at a clinic one afternoon.

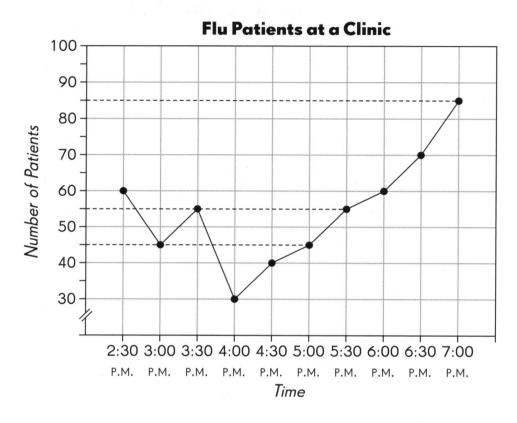

Flu Patients at a Clinic

12. How many patients were at the clinic at 5:30 P.M.? _____

13. How many patients were at the clinic at 6:30 P.M.? _____

14. During which half-hour interval did the number of patients at the clinic decrease the most? What was the decrease in the number of patients?

_____

_____

15. During which 1-hour interval did the number of patients at the clinic increase the most? What was the increase in the number of patients?

_____

_____

 **Put on Your Thinking Cap!**

Choose a graph type to display the data. Write *bar graph*, *line graph*, or *picture graph*. Explain your choice.

1.   The number of people at an amusement park who chose different rides

_____

_____

_____

_____

_____

_____

2.   The number of dogs visiting the veterinary hospital every hour

_____

_____

_____

_____

_____

_____

Follow the directions to create your own graph.

3. Use the newspaper, television, or internet to record the highest and lowest daily temperatures for a week. Complete the table with the data recorded.

Step 1

Day of the Week	Highest Daily Temperature	Lowest Daily Temperature
Monday		
Tuesday		
Wednesday		
Thursday		
Friday		
Saturday		
Sunday		

Next, complete the line graph using the same data. Use one color for the highest temperature and another color for the lowest temperature.

Step 2

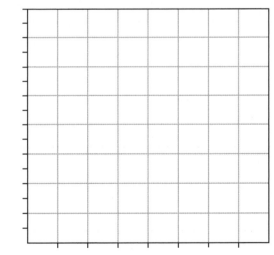

Day of the Week

Which representation makes the changes easier to see—a table or a line graph? Write about the advantages of each method of displaying data.

_____

_____

/50

Test Prep

for Chapters 1 to 4

Multiple Choice (10 × 2 points = 20 points)

Fill in the circle next to the correct answer.

1. In which of the following numbers is the digit 7 in the thousands place?

   Ⓐ 25,079   Ⓑ 33,780   Ⓒ 76,253   Ⓓ 97,201

2. When two numbers are rounded to the nearest hundred, the estimated sum is 5,200. One of the numbers is 1,578. What is the other number?

   Ⓐ 3,545   Ⓑ 3,645   Ⓒ 3,680   Ⓓ 3,700

3. What is 1,000 more than the difference between 7,309 and 9,037?

   Ⓐ 1,728   Ⓑ 2,728   Ⓒ 3,728   Ⓓ 4,728

4. Find the closest estimate of 39 × 649.

   Ⓐ 30 × 600   Ⓑ 30 × 700

   Ⓒ 40 × 600   Ⓓ 40 × 700

5. A number is a factor of 48. When this number is divided by 5, the remainder is 4. What is the number?

   Ⓐ 14   Ⓑ 16   Ⓒ 24   Ⓓ 34

6. Mrs. William's age is the fourth multiple of 12. If Mrs. William's age is 8 times her son's age, how old is her son? Her son's age is a factor of 30.

(A) 3   (B) 5   (C) 6   (D) 15

7. A number divided by 7 has 42 as its quotient and 5 as its remainder. What is this number?

(A) 6   (B) 11   (C) 289   (D) 299

8. $54 \times 123 = 6 \times 123 \times$?
Find the missing number.

(A) 3   (B) 6   (C) 9   (D) 18

Study the table and answer the questions.

The table shows four students' test scores.

Test Scores

Name	English	Mathematics	French	Science
Lionel	90	96	75	95
Shawna	75	90	86	80
Keith	64	45	80	40
Tara	82	86	65	89

9. What is the difference between Keith's highest and lowest scores?

(A) 5   (B) 24   (C) 40   (D) 55

10. How many more points did Lionel score than Tara in English?

(A) 8   (B) 15   (C) 18   (D) 26

Short Answer (10 × 2 points = 20 points)

Write your answers in the space given.

11. Write 67,098 in word form.

Answer: _____

12. A number is a multiple of 3. It is between 10 and 40.
It is also a factor of 45. What is the number?

Answer: _____

13. What is 414 less than the product of 319 and 6?

Answer: _____

14. What is the difference in the value of the digit 3 in 35,672 and
the value of the digit 3 in 43,980?

Answer: _____

Continue the pattern.

15.   20,388   21,388   22,488   23,688   24,988

Answer: _____   _____

Solve.

16. Mr. Garcia saves $834. He saves 6 times as much money as Mr. Larson.
How much does Mr. Larson save?

Answer: $_____

17. At the edge of a garden, 10 trees are planted in a row. The distance between the trees is the same. The distance between the first tree and the third tree is 12 feet. What is the distance between the first tree and the last tree?

Answer: _____

18. The cost of 3 action figures is $10. Ms. Bennett bought 72 action figures for her students. How much did she pay altogether?

Answer: $_____

19. Markers are sold in boxes of 7. Each box costs $8. Emily has $50. How many markers can she buy?

Answer: _____

20. A table and 4 identical chairs cost $865. If the table costs $589, what is the cost of each chair?

Answer: $_____

Extended Response (5 × 2 points = 10 points)

Solve. Show your work.

10

21. The line graph shows the distance Jared swam while swimming laps.

Distance Jared Swam

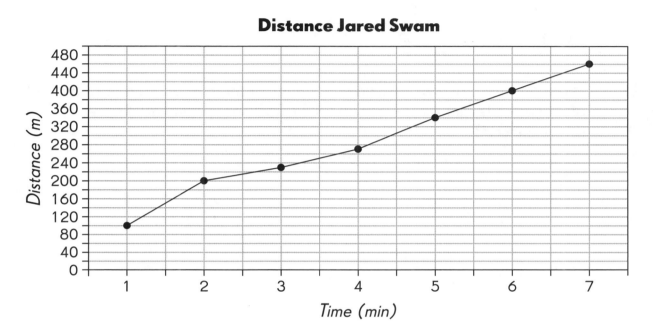

a. How many meters did Jared swim in 7 minutes?

b. During which 1-minute interval did Jared swim the shortest distance?

The ticket prices for a concert are shown in the table.

Concert Ticket Prices

	Price of Tickets
Adult	$5
Child	$2

22. There are twice as many children as adults at the concert. The total amount of money collected for the concert is $1,080. How many adults are at the concert?

23. Ms. Ervine has a basket of grapes.
If she gives 6 grapes to each of her students, she will have 2 grapes left.
If she gives 7 grapes to each of her students, she will have to buy 11 more grapes.

a. How many students does Ms. Ervine have?

b. How many grapes are in the basket?

Name: _____ Date: _____

CHAPTER 5 Data and Probability

Lesson 5.1 Average

Find the mean or average of each set of data.

The table shows the number of books Sophia borrowed from the library in four months.

Number of Books Borrowed

Month	March	April	May	June
Number of Books	12	10	8	14

1. | Step 1 | Find the total number of books.

_____ + _____ + _____ + _____ = _____

2. | Step 2 | Divide the total number of books by 4.

_____ ÷ 4 = _____

3. | Step 3 | Sophia borrowed an average of _____ books every month.

David has 5 sticks of different lengths.

26 in.
28 in.
30 in.
32 in.
34 in.

4. | Step 1 | Find the total length of the 5 sticks.

_____ in. + _____ in. + _____ in. +

_____ in. + _____ in. = _____ in.

5. | Step 2 | Divide the total length by 5.

_____ ÷ 5 = _____ in.

6. | Step 3 | The average length of the sticks is _____ inches.

Find the mean or average.

7.

The mean price of the sporting goods is $ _____.

Find the mean or average.

8.

The average volume of the jugs is _____ milliliters.

9.

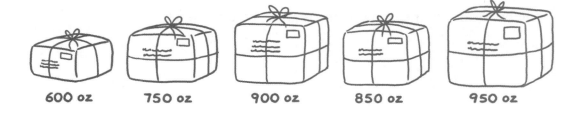

The mean weight of the parcels is _____ ounces.

10.

Jared's average test score is _____ points.

Answer the questions.

The table below shows the ages of 4 students.

Students' Ages

Name	Age
Alisha	15
Daniel	12
Jose	16
Matthew	17

11.   Which student is the same age as the average age?

12.   Which student(s) is/are older than the average age?

13.   Which student(s) is/are younger than the average age?

Solve.

14. The mean height of 3 boys is 150 centimeters. The mean height of 2 girls is 145 centimeters. Find the mean height of the 5 students.

15. An average of 1,896 people visited a museum in each month of March and April. Another 2,736 people visited the museum in May. What is the average number of visitors at the museum for these three months?

16. The average number of red, blue, and green beanbags in a store is 136. There are 30 more red beanbags than blue beanbags. There are 15 fewer green beanbags than blue beanbags. How many green beanbags are in the store? Use bar models to help you.

17. Joleen's total test score in English, math, and science is 264. She scores 1 point more in science than her average score and 5 points more in math than in science. What is her score in English?

Lesson 5.2   Median, Mode, and Range

Find the median, mode, range, and mean of each set of data.

7, 4, 9, 5, 10, 3, 4

1. Order the numbers from the least to the greatest: _____

2. Median: _____

3. Mode: _____

4. Range: _____

5. Mean: _____

18 ft, 16 ft, 16 ft, 12 ft, 19 ft, 15 ft

6. Order the distances from the least to the greatest: _____

7. Median: _____

8. Mode: _____

9. Range: _____

10. Mean: _____

Find the median, mode, range, and mean of the set of data.

35 yd, 38 yd, 30 yd, 38 yd, 34 yd

11.   Order the distances from the least to the greatest: _____

12.   Median: _____

13.   Mode: _____

14.   Range: _____

15.   Mean: _____

Find the range, mode, median, and mean.

The table shows the time it takes a group of students to travel to school.

Travel Time

Travel Time (minutes)	10	15	20	25	30
Number of Students	1	3	2	1	2

16.   The range of the travel times is _____ minutes.

17.   The mode of the travel times is _____ minutes.

18.   The median travel time is _____ minutes.

19.   The mean travel time is _____ minutes.

Use the line plot to complete the table.

The line plot shows the number of goals scored by each player in a soccer competition. Each ✗ represents one player.

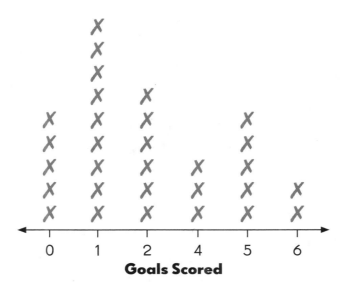

Goals Scored

20.   **Goals Scored**

Number of Goals	0	1	2	4	5	6
Number of Players	5					

Complete. Use the data in the line plot or the table.

21. _____ players were in the soccer competition.

22. The median number of goals scored is _____.

23. The mode of the set of data is _____.

24. The total number of goals scored is _____.

Fill in the blanks. Use the data in the line plot.

The line plot shows the points scored by students in a test.
Each ✗ represents one student.

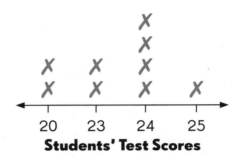

Students' Test Scores

25. _____ students took the test.

26. The mode of the set of data is _____.

27. The median of the set of data is _____.

28. The range of the set of data is _____.

29. The total number of points scored is _____.

30. The mean of the set of data is _____.

Name: _____   **Date:** _____

● **Make a line plot to show the data in the table.**

The table shows the foot length, in centimeters, of a group of students.

Foot Length

Length (cm)	14	16	18	20	22
Number of Students	3	2	2	4	1

31.   Make each **X** represent one student.

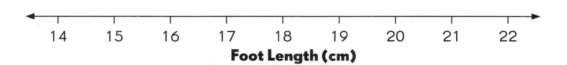

Foot Length (cm)

Complete. Use the data in your line plot.

32.   There are _____ students.

33.   The median of the set of data is _____ centimeters.

34.   The mode of the set of data is _____ centimeters.

35.   The range of the set of data is _____ centimeters.

Make a line plot to show the data in the table.

The school uses 8 buses. The table shows the number of students on each bus.

Number of Students on Each Bus

Number of Students	6	7	8
Number of Buses	3	2	3

36.   Make each ✗ represent one student.

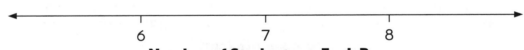

6   7   8
Number of Students on Each Bus

Complete. Use the data in your line plot.

37.   The median of the set of data is _____.

38.   The mode of the set of data is _____.

39.   The range of the set of data is _____.

40.   Find the mean number of students who are on each bus. _____

Lesson 5.3   Stem-and-Leaf Plots

Complete. Use the data in the stem-and-leaf plot.

The stem-and-leaf plot shows the time taken by 10 students to play the same video game.

Video Game Times (min)	
Stem	**Leaves**
2	8
3	0 0 0 5 5 8
4	0 5
5	9

2 | 8 = 28

1. The median, the middle time, is _____ minutes.

2. The mode, the most frequent time, is _____ minutes.

3. The range of the times is _____ minutes.

4. The outlier, the time farthest from the others, is _____ minutes.

Complete. Use the data in the stem-and-leaf plot.

The stem-and-leaf plot shows the heights of 8 children.

Heights of Children (in.)	
Stem	**Leaves**
2	4
3	0 3 4
4	2 5 5
5	9

2 | 4 = 24

5.   The modal height is _____ inches.

6.   The median height is _____ inches.

7.   The range of the heights is _____ inches.

8.   The outlier is _____ inches.

9.   The mean height is _____ inches.

Complete. Use the data in the stem-and-leaf plot.

9 motorists were surveyed to find the amount of money they spend every month on gas.

Amount Spent on Gas ($)	
Stem	**Leaves**
20	5
26	4 8
27	5 5 6
28	4
29	2
30	9

20 | 5 = 205

10. The median of the set of data is $ _____.

11. The mode of the set of data is $ _____.

12. The range of the set of data is $ _____.

13. The outlier of the set of data is $ _____.

14. The mean of the set of data is $ _____.

Make a stem-and-leaf plot to show the data.

The data shows the number of dogs walked by a pet service in 9 days.

10, 25, 32, 25, 27, 33, 26, 28, 28

15.

Number of Dogs Walked	
Stem	**Leaves**

____ | ____ = ____

Complete. Use the data in the stem-and-leaf plot.

16. The modes of the set of data are _____ and _____.

17. The median of the set of data is _____.

18. The range of the set of data is _____.

19. The average of the set of data is _____.

20. The number of dogs walked was less than 30 on _____ days.

Lesson 5.4   Outcomes

**Complete. Write *more likely, less likely, certain, impossible,*
or *equally likely.***

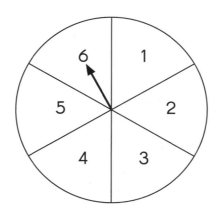

1.   It is _____ that the spinner will land on 6.

2.   It is _____ that the spinner will land on a number from 1 to 6.

3.   It is _____ that the spinner will land on a number less than 5.

4.   It is _____ that the spinner will land on 8.

5.   It is _____ that the spinner will land on an even or an odd number.

**Write *more likely, less likely, certain, impossible,* or *equally likely*
for each of these statements.**

6.   I will go to college. _____

7.   I will grow 5 inches this week. _____

8.   My father is older than me. _____

9.   A coin will land on heads when it is tossed. _____

10.   A coin will land on heads or tails when it is tossed. _____

Write the number of possible outcomes.

 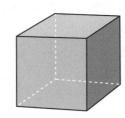 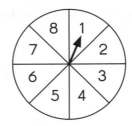

11.   There are _____ possible outcomes when a coin is tossed.

12.   There are _____ possible outcomes when the cube is tossed.

13.   The spinner has _____ possible outcomes.

Study the data in the table. Write *more likely, less likely, certain, impossible,* or *equally likely* to describe each outcome.

Number of Caps in Three Boxes

Color of Caps	Box A	Box B	Box C
Orange	9	0	6
Purple	3	8	6
Red	3	6	4

14.   A purple cap is drawn from Box A. _____

15.   An orange cap is drawn from Box B. _____

16.   An orange or purple cap is drawn from Box C. _____

17.   A green cap is drawn from Box C. _____

Lesson 5.5   Probability as a Fraction

Find the probability as a fraction in simplest form.

1.   Aleesha spins the spinner once. She wants to land on a number greater than 4. What is the probability of a favorable outcome?

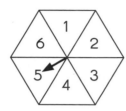

    a.   There are _____ favorable outcomes.

    b.   There are _____ possible outcomes.

    c.   Probability of a favorable outcome = ⬜

                           = ⬜

Aleesha spins the spinner again.

2.   What is the probability that the spinner will land on 4? ⬜

3.   What is the probability that the spinner will land on an even number? ⬜

4.   What is the probability that the spinner will land on a number less than 5? ⬜

5.   What is the probability that the spinner will land on a number less than 7? ⬜

Find the probability of each outcome on the number line.
Write each probability as a fraction in simplest form.
**Then describe the outcome as *more likely, less likely, certain, impossible,*
or *equally likely*.**

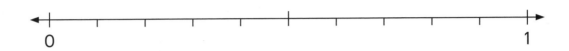

0   1

A bag contains 3 red balls, 4 blue balls, 2 green balls, and 1 yellow ball.
Find the probability of drawing

6.   a yellow ball:

It is _____ that a yellow ball will be drawn from the bag.

7.   a green ball:

It is _____ that a green ball will be drawn from the bag.

8.   a yellow ball or a green ball:

It is _____ that a yellow or a green ball will be drawn
from the bag.

9.   a green ball, a red ball, or a blue ball:

It is _____ that a green, red, or a blue ball will be drawn
from the bag.

Find the probability as a fraction in simplest form.

A set of 12 cards is numbered from 1 to 12.

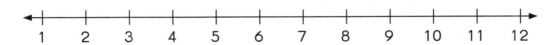

Find the probability of drawing

10. a card greater than 7: ☐

11. an odd number: ☐

12. a card less than 10: ☐

13. an even number: ☐

14. a 1-digit number: ☐

15. a 2-digit number: ☐

Draw.

A spinner has 8 equal parts. Four of the parts are green, 2 of the parts are purple, and the last 2 parts are blue and red.

16. Draw the spinner with the correct colored parts.

Find the probability as a fraction in simplest form.

Find the probability of landing on

17. purple:

18. green:

19. blue or red:

20. yellow:

Lesson 5.6   Real-World Problems: Data and Probability

Solve. Show your work.

1. In a basketball game, Miguel, Tony, Jason, and Finch scored an average of 16 points. Jason scored 20 points and Finch scored 8 points. How many points did Miguel and Tony score altogether?

2. Three dolphins are born at a zoo. The total weight of the baby dolphins is 196 pounds. The first baby dolphin weighs 88 pounds. What is the mean weight of the other two dolphins?

3. Adrian, Dakota, and Calvin made an average of 52 snacks. Adrian and Dakota made an average of 61 snacks. Dakota and Calvin made an average of 44 snacks. How many snacks did each of them make?

4. A group of 100 students took a quiz. Their average score was 76 points. If the average score for the boys was 80 points and the average score for the girls was 70 points, how many girls participated in the quiz?

Use the data to complete the table and the line plot.

5. Complete the table with the number of letters in each name.

Number of Letters

Name	Number of Letters
Jessica	
Brenda	
Carl	
Fiona	
Jeremy	
Barry	
Nicole	
Zoe	
Ann	

a. Make a line plot to show the data.

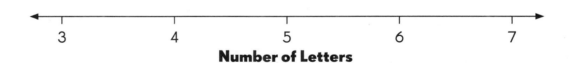

Number of Letters

b. Find the mode.

c. Find the range.

d. Find the mean.

e. Ann forgot to add her full name, Annemarie, to the set of data. Does this change the mode, range, or mean?

Solve. Use the data in the stem-and-leaf plot. Show your work.

The data shows the scores from a bowling tournament.

Bowling Scores	
Stem	**Leaves**
4	6
5	4
6	3
7	
8	1 7 7
9	2 8

$4 \mid 6 = 46$

6. What is the modal score?

7. What is the median score?

8. What is the range of the scores?

9. What is the mean score?

10. Another player joins the tournament. The new mean score is 76. What is the new player's score?

11.   20 students are in a classroom. If students leave randomly, the probability that the first student to leave the classroom is a girl is $\frac{3}{5}$. How many girls are there?

12.   A bag contains 3 red crayons, 2 blue crayons, 4 yellow crayons, and 3 green crayons. A crayon is drawn from the bag.

   a.   Find the probability that the crayon is a yellow crayon.

   b.   Find the probability that the crayon is a red or a green crayon.

13. A parking lot has 20 vehicles in it. There are 8 cars, 4 buses, 6 motorcycles, and 2 vans. The first vehicle that leaves the parking lot is a car.
If vehicles leave randomly, what is the probability that the second vehicle to leave is a bus?

14. The mean of Susan's math and science scores is 74 points. The mean of her math and English scores is 83 points. How many more points did Susan score in English than in science?

Put on Your Thinking Cap!

1. Mr. Peterson sells an average of 147 newspapers on each weekday, and an average of 217 newspapers on each day of the weekend. What is the average number of newspapers Mr. Peterson is able to sell on each day of the week?

2. Pauline scores an average of 78 points on three tests.
    How many points will Pauline need to score on her next test to raise her average score to 82 points?

3. Box B contains $\frac{1}{2}$ as many paper clips as Box A. Box C contains $\frac{2}{3}$ as many paper clips as Box B. The average number of paper clips in each box is 88. How many paper clips are in Box A?

4. Mr. Clarkson and Ms. Rose had an average of $180. After Mr. Clarkson spent $73 and Ms. Rose received $38 from her father, Mr. Clarkson had $\frac{1}{4}$ as much money as Ms. Rose. How much money did each have at first?

5. Tracy, Joyce, Mark, and Sarah collect key chains. They have an average of 68 key chains. Tracy has 78 key chains. Joyce has half as many key chains as Mark. Sarah has 28 fewer key chains than the total number of key chains that Joyce and Mark have. How many key chains does Mark have?

6. A group of students calculated their average score at a spelling bee. They realized that if one of them scored 9 more points, their average score would be 81 points. If one of them scored 3 points less, their average score would be 78 points. How many students were in the group?

7.   The mean height of Jason, Peter, and Edward is 145 centimeters. Jason is
7 centimeters taller than Peter. Peter is 10 centimeters taller than Edward.
What is each boy's height?

6 Fractions and Mixed Numbers

Lesson 6.1   Adding Fractions

Find the equivalent fraction. Complete the model and add the fractions.

1. $\dfrac{1}{9} + \dfrac{2}{3} = \dfrac{\square}{\square} + \dfrac{\square}{\square} = \square$

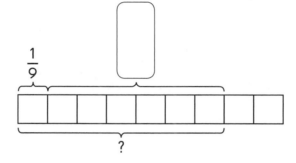

2. $\dfrac{1}{2} + \dfrac{1}{6} = \dfrac{\square}{\square} + \dfrac{\square}{\square} = \square = \square$

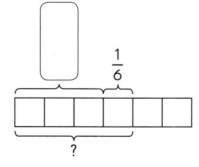

Name: _____ **Date:** _____

Add. Write each answer in simplest form.

3. $\frac{2}{5} + \frac{1}{10} = \frac{\square}{\square} + \frac{\square}{\square} = \square = \square$

4. $\frac{2}{3} + \frac{2}{12} = \frac{\square}{\square} + \frac{\square}{\square} = \square = \square$

5. Add $\frac{1}{4}$ and $\frac{1}{12}$.

6. Add $\frac{1}{4}$ to your answer in Exercise 5.

7. Add $\frac{1}{3}$ and $\frac{1}{6}$.

8. Add $\frac{1}{6}$ to your answer in Exercise 7.

9. What is the sum of $\frac{1}{8}$, $\frac{1}{4}$, and $\frac{2}{4}$?

10. What is the sum of $\frac{1}{6}$, $\frac{3}{18}$, and $\frac{4}{9}$?

Lesson 6.2 Subtracting Fractions

Find the equivalent fraction. Complete the model. Then subtract.

1. $\dfrac{5}{6} - \dfrac{1}{2} = \dfrac{\square}{\square} - \dfrac{\square}{\square} = \square = \square$

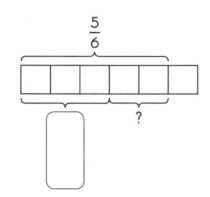

2. $\dfrac{7}{12} - \dfrac{1}{3} = \dfrac{\square}{\square} - \dfrac{\square}{\square} = \square = \square$

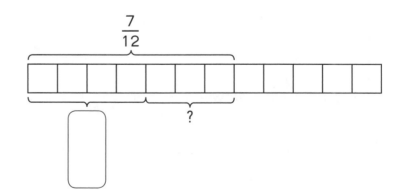

Subtract. Write each answer in simplest form.

3. $\dfrac{3}{4} - \dfrac{5}{12} = \dfrac{\boxed{}}{\boxed{}} - \dfrac{\boxed{}}{\boxed{}} = \boxed{} = \boxed{}$

4. $\dfrac{4}{5} - \dfrac{3}{10} = \dfrac{\boxed{}}{\boxed{}} - \dfrac{\boxed{}}{\boxed{}} = \boxed{} = \boxed{}$

5. $1 - \dfrac{7}{12} - \dfrac{1}{4} = \boxed{} = \boxed{}$

6. $1 - \dfrac{6}{16} - \dfrac{4}{8} = \boxed{} = \boxed{}$

7. Subtract $\dfrac{1}{3}$ from $\dfrac{5}{6}$.

8. Subtract $\dfrac{5}{6}$ from $\dfrac{11}{12}$.

9. The difference between $\dfrac{7}{10}$ and $\dfrac{3}{5}$ is $\boxed{}$.

10. The difference between 1 and $\dfrac{7}{8}$ is $\boxed{}$.

Lesson 6.3   Mixed Numbers

Write a mixed number for each model.

1.

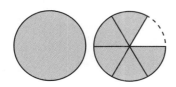

$$1 + \frac{5}{6} = \boxed{}$$

2.

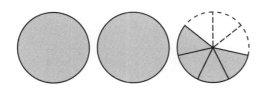

$$3 + \frac{3}{8} = \boxed{}$$

3.

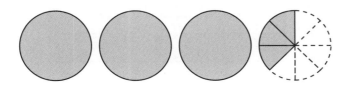

$$2 + \frac{4}{7} = \boxed{}$$

4.

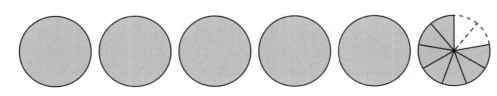

$$5 + \frac{7}{9} = \boxed{}$$

Name: _____   Date: _____

Write a mixed number for each model.

5.

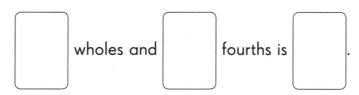

☐ wholes and ☐ fourths is ☐ .

6.

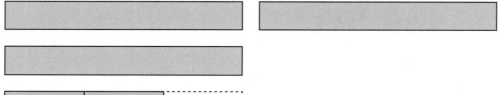

☐ wholes and ☐ sixths is ☐ .

7.

☐ wholes and ☐ thirds is ☐ .

Write a mixed number for each of the following.

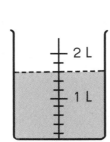

8.   The volume of water in the container is _____ liters.

9.   The weight of five oranges is _____ pounds.

Write each answer as a mixed number.

10. $2 + \dfrac{3}{5} =$ ☐

11. $\dfrac{5}{8} + 4 =$ ☐

12. $3 + \dfrac{4}{9} =$ ☐

13. $5 + \dfrac{7}{12} =$ ☐

14. $\dfrac{1}{6} + 2 =$ ☐

15. $\dfrac{3}{10} + 4 =$ ☐

Simplify.

16. $2\dfrac{6}{8} =$ ☐

17. $1\dfrac{4}{10} =$ ☐

18. $4\dfrac{3}{9} =$ ☐

19. $3\dfrac{9}{12} =$ ☐

Write the correct fraction or mixed number in each box.
Express each answer in simplest form.

20.

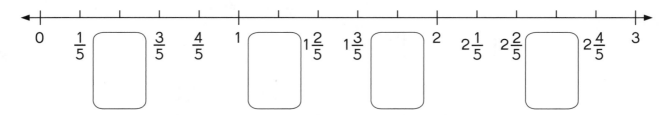

21.

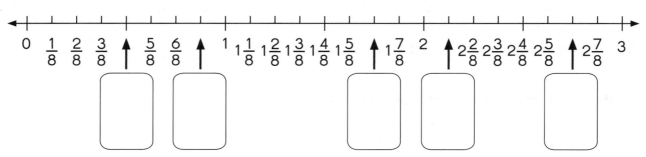

22.

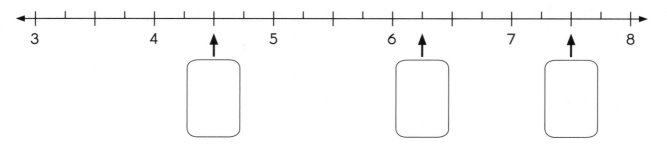

23.

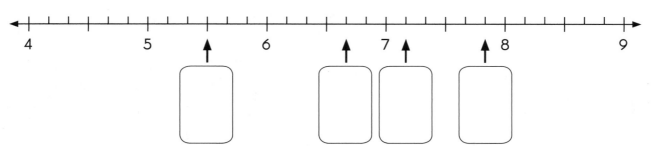

Lesson 6.4   Improper Fractions

Write each mixed number as an improper fraction.

1.

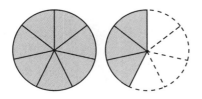

    a. $1 =$ _____ sevenths

    b. $\frac{3}{7} =$ _____ sevenths

    c. $1\frac{3}{7} =$ _____ sevenths

    d. $=$ ☐

2.

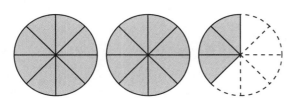

    a. $2 =$ _____ eighths

    b. $\frac{3}{8} =$ _____ eighths

    c. $2\frac{3}{8} =$ _____ eighths

    d. $=$ ☐

3.

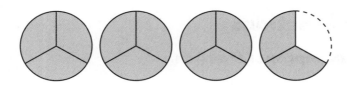

    a. $3 = $ _____ thirds

    b. $\frac{2}{3} = $ _____ thirds

    c. $3\frac{2}{3} = $ _____ thirds

    d. $= \boxed{}$

Write the improper fractions for the shaded parts.

4.

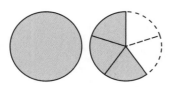

     $1\frac{3}{5} = \boxed{}$

5.

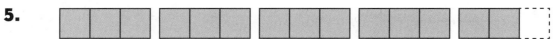

     $4\frac{2}{3} = \boxed{}$

6.

     $6\frac{1}{2} = \boxed{}$

Name: _____ Date: _____

● **Write a mixed number and an improper fraction for each model.**

7.

Mixed number: ☐   Improper fraction: ☐

8.

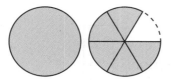

Mixed number: ☐   Improper fraction: ☐

9.

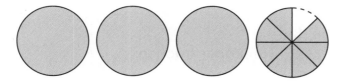

Mixed number: ☐   Improper fraction: ☐

10.

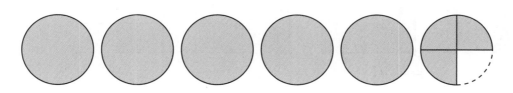

Mixed number: ☐   Improper fraction: ☐

11.

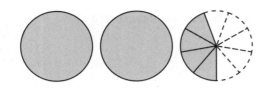

Mixed number: ☐   Improper fraction: ☐

12.

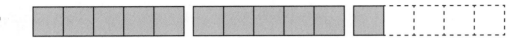

Mixed number: ☐   Improper fraction: ☐

13.

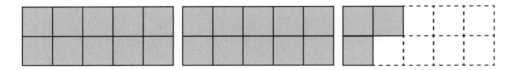

Mixed number: ☐   Improper fraction: ☐

14.

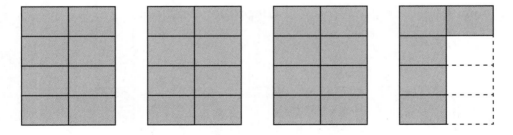

Mixed number: ☐   Improper fraction: ☐

Write the missing improper fraction in each box.
Express each answer in simplest form.

15.

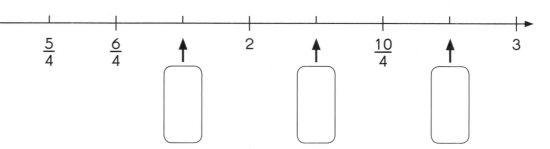

16.

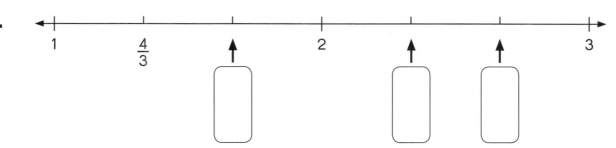

17.

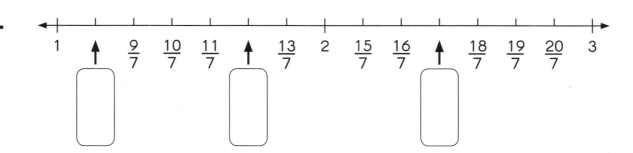

18.

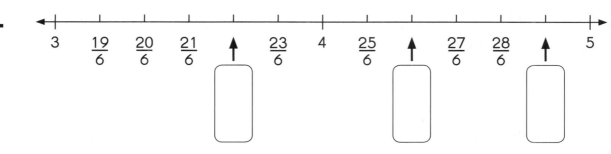

19.

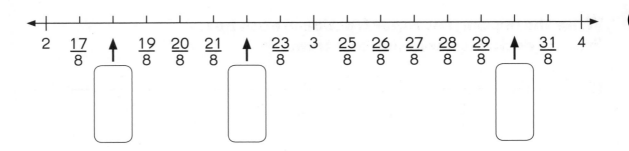

20.

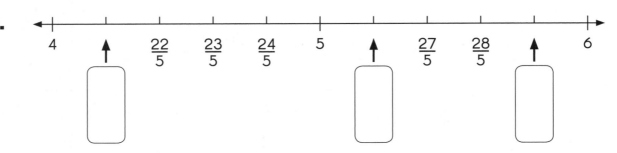

21.

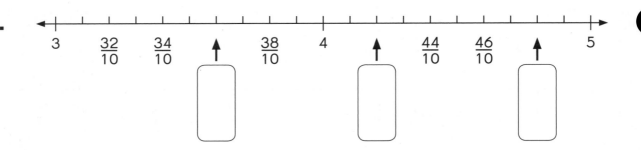

22.

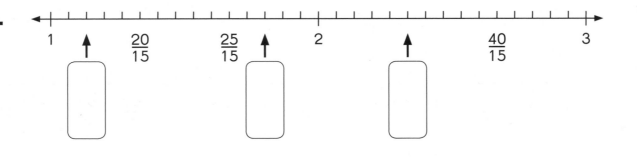

Lesson 6.5   Renaming Improper Fractions and Mixed Numbers

Express each improper fraction as a mixed number.

1. $\dfrac{11}{2} = \dfrac{10}{2} + \dfrac{1}{2}$

$= 5 + \dfrac{\boxed{}}{2}$

$= 5\,\dfrac{\boxed{}}{2}$

2. $\dfrac{20}{3} = \dfrac{18}{3} + \dfrac{2}{3}$

$= 6 + \dfrac{\boxed{}}{3}$

$= 6\,\dfrac{\boxed{}}{3}$

3. $\dfrac{13}{4} = \dfrac{\boxed{}}{4} + \dfrac{\boxed{}}{4}$

$= 3 + \dfrac{\boxed{}}{4}$

$= 3\,\dfrac{\boxed{}}{4}$

4. $\dfrac{23}{5} = \dfrac{\boxed{}}{5} + \dfrac{\boxed{}}{5}$

$= 4 + \dfrac{\boxed{}}{5}$

$= 4\,\dfrac{\boxed{}}{5}$

5. $\dfrac{27}{10} = \dfrac{\boxed{}}{10} + \dfrac{\boxed{}}{10}$

$= \boxed{} + \dfrac{\boxed{}}{10}$

$= \boxed{}$

6. $\dfrac{26}{7} = \dfrac{\boxed{}}{7} + \dfrac{\boxed{}}{7}$

$= \boxed{} + \dfrac{\boxed{}}{7}$

$= \boxed{}$

Express each improper fraction as a mixed number in simplest form.

7. $\dfrac{16}{6} = 2 + \dfrac{\boxed{}}{6}$

   $= \boxed{}$

8. $\dfrac{20}{8} = 2 + \dfrac{\boxed{}}{8}$

   $= \boxed{}$

9. $\dfrac{15}{2} = \boxed{}$

10. $\dfrac{18}{10} = \boxed{}$

11. $\dfrac{21}{9} = \boxed{}$

12. $\dfrac{15}{12} = \boxed{}$

13. $\dfrac{22}{7} = \boxed{}$

14. $\dfrac{36}{6} = \boxed{}$

15. $\dfrac{30}{4} = \boxed{}$

16. $\dfrac{42}{5} = \boxed{}$

17. $\dfrac{28}{13} = \boxed{}$

18. $\dfrac{48}{15} = \boxed{}$

Express each mixed number as an improper fraction.

19. $3\frac{2}{3} = 3 + \frac{2}{3}$

$= \dfrac{\boxed{}}{3} + \dfrac{2}{3}$

$= \dfrac{\boxed{}}{3}$

20. $1\frac{1}{4} = 1 + \frac{1}{4}$

$= \dfrac{\boxed{}}{4} + \dfrac{1}{4}$

$= \dfrac{\boxed{}}{4}$

21. $2\frac{3}{5} = \dfrac{\boxed{}}{5} + \dfrac{3}{5}$

$= \dfrac{\boxed{}}{5}$

22. $2\frac{5}{6} = \dfrac{\boxed{}}{6} + \dfrac{5}{6}$

$= \dfrac{\boxed{}}{6}$

23. $2\frac{4}{7} = \dfrac{\boxed{}}{7} + \dfrac{\boxed{}}{7}$

$= \dfrac{\boxed{}}{9}$

24. $2\frac{2}{9} = \dfrac{\boxed{}}{9} + \dfrac{\boxed{}}{9}$

$= \dfrac{\boxed{}}{9}$

Express each mixed number as an improper fraction.

25. $4\frac{1}{3} = $ ☐

26. $2\frac{3}{10} = $ ☐

27. $1\frac{2}{7} = $ ☐

28. $1\frac{5}{9} = $ ☐

29. $2\frac{1}{4} = $ ☐

30. $2\frac{5}{12} = $ ☐

31. $1\frac{3}{10} = $ ☐

32. $1\frac{2}{11} = $ ☐

33. $5\frac{4}{5} = $ ☐

34. $3\frac{8}{9} = $ ☐

35. $6\frac{1}{5} = $ ☐

36. $7\frac{2}{7} = $ ☐

Lesson 6.6 Renaming Whole Numbers when Adding and Subtracting Fractions

Add. Express each answer as a mixed number in simplest form.

1. $\frac{5}{9} + \frac{2}{3} =$

2. $\frac{3}{4} + \frac{11}{12} =$

3. $\frac{1}{2} + \frac{7}{8} =$

4. $\frac{1}{6} + \frac{2}{3} =$

5. $\frac{7}{10} + \frac{4}{5} =$

6. $\frac{5}{12} + \frac{2}{3} =$

7. $\frac{5}{6} + \frac{7}{12} =$

8. $\frac{6}{8} + \frac{3}{4} =$

9. $\frac{5}{12} + \frac{1}{2} + \frac{2}{3} =$

10. $\frac{1}{2} + \frac{3}{8} + \frac{3}{4} =$

Subtract. Express each answer as a mixed number in simplest form.

11. $3 - \dfrac{7}{12} =$

12. $4 - \dfrac{8}{9} =$

13. $2 - \dfrac{4}{5} =$

14. $5 - \dfrac{2}{3} =$

15. $3 - \dfrac{1}{6} - \dfrac{1}{3} =$

16. $4 - \dfrac{1}{4} - \dfrac{1}{2} =$

17. $6 - \dfrac{2}{5} - \dfrac{3}{10} =$

18. $3 - \dfrac{2}{7} - \dfrac{5}{14} =$

19. $2 - \dfrac{5}{12} - \dfrac{1}{6} =$

20. $5 - \dfrac{2}{3} - \dfrac{2}{9} =$

Lesson 6.7   Fraction of a Set

What fraction of each set of objects is shaded? Express your answer in simplest form.

1.

2.

3.

4.

Name: _____ **Date:** _____

Use a model to help you answer each question.

Example

What is $\frac{3}{4}$ of 24?

4 units = 24
1 unit = 6
3 units = 6 × 3 = 18

So, $\frac{3}{4}$ of 24 = 18.

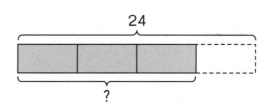

5. What is $\frac{4}{5}$ of 30?

5 units = _____

1 unit = _____

4 units = _____

So, $\frac{4}{5}$ of 30 = _____.

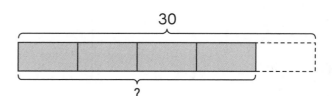

6. What is $\frac{5}{6}$ of 48?

7. What is $\frac{5}{12}$ of 60?

Solve.

8. $\frac{2}{3} \times 45$

$\frac{2}{3}$ of 45 is _____.

9. $\frac{4}{9} \times 36$

$\frac{4}{9}$ of 36 is _____.

10. $\frac{2}{7} \times 35$

11. $\frac{3}{8} \times 32$

Lesson 6.8   Real-World Problems: Fractions

Solve. Show your work.

1. Arthur had $90. He spent $40 and gave $20 to his brother.
    What fraction of Arthur's money is left?

2. A baker has 20 pounds of sugar. He uses $\frac{3}{4}$ of the sugar to bake muffins.
    How much sugar does he have left?

3. Mya buys 6 goldfish and 4 angelfish.
  a. What fraction of the fish are goldfish?

  b. Mya buys 2 more goldfish. What fraction of the fish are angelfish?

4. Cheryl spends $\frac{3}{10}$ of her savings on a book, and $\frac{2}{5}$ of it on a pen. What fraction of her savings does Cheryl spend?

5. Of the vehicles on the road, $\frac{1}{2}$ are cars and $\frac{1}{8}$ are motorcycles. What fraction of the vehicles are not cars or motorcycles?

6. Allie's plant has a height of 6 meters. Rajon's plant grows $\frac{3}{10}$ meter higher. How high does Rajon's plant grow?

7. There are 10 packets of ham. Of the packets, $\frac{2}{5}$ are turkey ham. Each packet of turkey ham weighs $\frac{1}{3}$ pound. What is the total weight of the turkey ham?

8. Carla spends $\frac{6}{4}$ hours exercising every day for 12 days. She spends $\frac{1}{2}$ of her exercise time every day lifting weights. How much time does Carla spend lifting weights during the 12 days?

 Put on Your Thinking Cap!

1. Justin buys a pair of pants and a shirt. He spends $\frac{2}{5}$ of the total money on the shirt. He pays $27 for the pair of pants. How much does Justin pay for the shirt?

2. Of all the peppers the chef has, $\frac{5}{7}$ are red and the rest are green. The chef has a total of 34 green peppers. How many peppers does she have altogether?

3. A basket $\frac{1}{2}$ full of apples weighs 8 pounds. When the basket is filled with apples, it weighs 11 pounds. What is the weight of the empty basket?

4. Write the fractions $\frac{2}{9}$, $\frac{1}{3}$, $\frac{1}{6}$, $\frac{7}{18}$, $\frac{4}{9}$, and $\frac{5}{18}$ in the boxes. The three fractions on each side of the triangle should have a sum of 1.

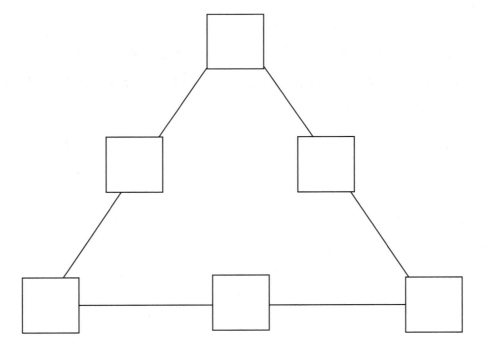

Mid-Year Test

Multiple Choice (20 × 2 points = 40 points)

Fill in the circle next to the correct answer.

1. Eighty-nine thousand, nine hundred eight in standard form is

(A) 8,998   (B) 89,098   (C) 89,908   (D) 89,980

2. 28 thousands 6 hundreds 8 ones in expanded form is

(A) 20,000 + 80 + 60 + 8

(B) 20,000 + 800 + 600 + 8

(C) 20,000 + 8,000 + 60 + 8

(D) 20,000 + 8,000 + 600 + 8

3. The value of the digit 7 in 79,365 is

(A) 70 hundreds   (B) 7 ten thousands

(C) 7 thousands   (D) 70 ten thousands

4. Which of the following is the best estimate of 498 × 63?

(A) 400 × 60   (B) 400 × 70   (C) 500 × 60   (D) 500 × 70

5. Find the product of 379 and 36. The answer rounded to the nearest hundred is

(A) 13,000   (B) 13,600   (C) 13,700   (D) 14,000

6. Multiply 48 by 28. Then divide the product by 4.

(A) 322   (B) 336   (C) 1,228   (D) 334

7. Which pair of numbers has a common factor of 6?

(A) 3 and 6   (B) 36 and 76   (C) 54 and 84   (D) 48 and 64

8. The product of the fourth multiple of 9 and the sixth multiple of 7 is

(A) 36   (B) 42   (C) 63   (D) 1,512

9. Keith's age is between 30 and 60 years. It is also a multiple of 6.
Sean's age is a factor of 24. Keith's age is 4 times Sean's age.
How old is Sean?

(A) 4   (B) 6   (C) 8   (D) 12

The line graph shows the number of visitors at a carnival one day.

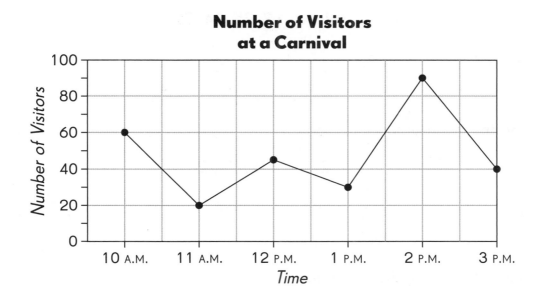

Number of Visitors at a Carnival

10. At what time was the number of visitors twice as many as the number of visitors at 1 P.M.?

(A) 10 A.M.   (B) 11 A.M.   (C) 2 P.M.   (D) 3 P.M.

11. At what time was the number of visitors half the number of visitors at 2 P.M.?

(A) 10 A.M.   (B) 12 P.M.   (C) 1 P.M.   (D) 3 P.M.

12. Each visitor was charged $20. What was the total amount of money collected over the six hours?

(A) $285   (B) $800   (C) $2,850   (D) $5,700

13. There were 49 fewer male visitors than female visitors in total. How many male visitors were at the carnival?

(A) 113   (B) 118   (C) 167   (D) 236

14. Find the median of the set of data.

$$12, 18, 16, 25, 14, 20, 22$$

(A) 14   (B) 16   (C) 18   (D) 25

15. Find the mean of the set of data.

$$26, 22, 18, 24, 28, 20$$

(A) 22   (B) 23   (C) 24   (D) 25

16. Find the mode of the set of data.

$$7, 9, 10, 7, 5, 12, 11, 7, 8, 10$$

(A) 7   (B) 8   (C) 9   (D) 10

17. The sum of $\frac{5}{6}$ and $\frac{2}{3}$ is

(A) $\frac{7}{9}$ (B) $1\frac{1}{3}$ (C) $1\frac{1}{6}$ (D) $1\frac{1}{2}$

18. What fraction of the figure is shaded?

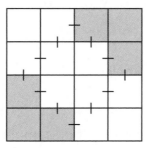

(A) $\frac{3}{16}$ (B) $\frac{1}{4}$ (C) $\frac{3}{8}$ (D) $\frac{5}{8}$

19. The weight of a cabbage is three times that of an orange.

The weight of the orange is $\frac{3}{10}$ pound. How much heavier is the cabbage?

(A) $\frac{3}{10}$ lb   (B) $\frac{3}{5}$ lb   (C) $\frac{9}{10}$ lb   (D) $1\frac{1}{15}$ lb

20. A class has 42 students. $\frac{2}{7}$ of the students scored an A on a history test. How many students did not score an A?

(A) 6   (B) 12   (C) 30   (D) 36

Short Answer (20 × 2 points = 40 points)

Write your answer in the space given.

21. Find the sum of 2,837, 3,759 and 5,528. What is the digit in the hundreds place?

Answer: _____

22. Divide 2,597 by 7.

Answer: _____

23.

1	2	0	3	8

Find the least 5-digit odd number that can be formed from the digits.

Answer: _____

24. Continue the number pattern.

3 6 12 15 30 33 66 _____ _____

Answer: _____

25. When the spinner is spun, what is the probability that it will land on a multiple of 2?

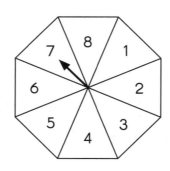

Answer: _____

The stem-and-leaf plot shows the height, in centimeters, of 10 students in a class.

Heights of Students	
Stem	**Leaves**
12	9
13	0 2 3 5 8
14	1 2 3
15	6

12 | 9 = 129

26. Find the range and outlier of the set of data.

Answer: _____

_____

27. What fraction of the flowers is not shaded?

Answer: _____

28. Ms. Jackson draws a line plot to show the long-jump results of her students during a Physical Education class. Each ✗ represents one student.

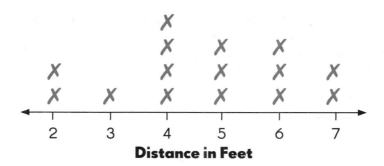

Find the mode of the set of data.

Answer: _____

29. What is 5,000 more than the product of 297 and 48?

Answer: _____

30. 1,350 × 49 = ⬚

⬚ + 49 = 66,199

What is the missing number in the box?

Answer: _____

31. A number is multiplied by 4, and then its product is divided by 8. The quotient obtained is 39. What is the number?

Answer: _____

The table below shows the number of people (rounded to the nearest hundred) at the museum from Monday to Saturday.

Number of Visitors at the Museum

Day	Monday	Tuesday	Wednesday	Thursday	Friday	Saturday
Number of People	1,200	900	800	1,500	800	600

Complete. Use the data in the table.

32. What is the greatest number of people who could have visited the museum on Thursday?

Answer: _____

33. On which day were there about half as many people visiting the museum as on Monday?

Answer: _____

34. What is the total number of people (rounded to the nearest hundred) visiting the museum from Monday to Saturday?

Answer: _____

35. About how many more people visited the museum on Tuesday than on Friday?

Answer: _____

Answer the questions.

36. A painter mixes $\frac{3}{4}$ liter of blue paint with $\frac{5}{12}$ liter of yellow paint. How many liters of green paint does he get?

Answer: _____

37. Katy gives $\frac{1}{3}$ of her crayons to her sister, and $\frac{2}{9}$ to her brother. What fraction of the crayons does she have left?

Answer: _____

38. $\frac{2}{5}$ of the students at Kennedy High are girls. There are 1,482 boys in the school. How many students are at Kennedy High?

Answer: _____

39. Sakina receives 200 tacos to distribute in her school. Alisha receives half as many tacos as Sakina. How many tacos do they receive in all?

Answer: _____

40. A bag contains only 50¢ coins and $1 bills. The total amount of money in the bag is $36. If there are twice as many 50¢ coins as $1 bills, how many 50¢ coins are in the bag?

Answer: _____

Extended Response (5 × 4 points = 20 points)

Solve. Show your work.

41. Basket A contains 920 plums, and Basket B contains 580 plums.
Matthew moves some plums from Basket A to Basket B so that
the two baskets have an equal number of plums.
How many plums does Matthew move from Basket A to Basket B?

42. Michael pays $3,328 for 2 computers and 2 printers.
Each computer costs three times as much as each printer.
a. How much does each printer cost?

b. How much does each computer cost?

43.   Mr. Carlos buys 1,080 apples. $\frac{1}{9}$ of the apples are rotten. He sells the rest at $2 for 10 apples. How much does he earn from the sale?

44.   Ahmad, Barry, and Tara collected some seashells. Ahmad collected $\frac{1}{6}$ of the seashells, Barry collected $\frac{1}{2}$ of the seashells, and the rest were collected by Tara. Tara collected 76 seashells.
How many seashells did they collect in all?

45. At the first stop on a bus route, $\frac{1}{3}$ of the passengers get off, and 8 people board the bus. At the second stop, $\frac{1}{4}$ of the passengers get off, and 9 people board the bus. If there are 45 passengers on the bus now, how many passengers started the trip?

Answers

Chapter 1

Lesson 1.1 (Part 1)

1. 38,600   2. 80,240   3. 46,059
4. 20,012   5. 73,001   6. 13,513
7. seventy-three thousand, two hundred forty-six
8. eleven thousand, two hundred eighty
9. sixty thousand, fifty-four
10. nineteen thousand, seven hundred seven
11. fifty-five thousand, fifty-five
12. forty-eight thousand, three hundred
13. ninety thousand, nine hundred ninety
14. 69,500; 70,000
15. 62,000; 65,000
16. 57,000; 67,000
17. fifty; 8   18. thousand; 2
19. three; 6   20. forty; 0

Accept all possible answers for Q21 and Q22.

21. 86,037   22. 30,786
23. 30,678   24. 87,630
25. 30,678   26. 87,603
27. 40,529   28. 54,209
29. 20,459   30. 20,594
31. 94,205   32. 95,420

Lesson 1.1 (Part 2)

1. thousands   2. ones
3. ten thousands 4. tens
5. hundreds   6. 400
7. 5   8. 90,000
9. 80   10. 1,000
11. 4   12. 20
13. 7   14. 8
15. thousands   16. tens
17. 90,000   18. ones
19. 6,000   20. 7; 700
21. 3; 4   22. 7; 8; 6
23. ten thousands; thousands; hundreds; 8
24. 9 ten thousands; 8 hundreds; tens

25. 20,000; 300; 20
26. 7,000; 80
27. 2,000; 600; 30
28. 50,000; 6,000; 60
29. 90,000; 9,000; 800; 50
30. 89,346   31. 3,421

Lesson 1.2

1. >   2. <   3. <   4. >
5. 26,653   6. 91,111
7. 91,111   8. 60,002
9. 61,253; 61,352; 61,532
10. 78,631; 78,061; 76,138
11. 76,250   12. 78,900
13. 56,500   14. 45,990
15. 32,120   16. 43,500
17. 22,800   18. 62,000
19. 31,080; 31,280
    Rule: Add 200.
20. 58,700; 60,200
    Rule: Add 1,500.
21. 65,120; 65,720
    Rule: Add 600 and then add 400.
22. 22,000; 26,000
    Rule: Multiply the difference between the last
    two numbers by 2. Then add the product to the
    last number.

Put on Your Thinking Cap!

Strategy: Logical reasoning
1. 86,420   2. 400   3. 80,000
Thinking skill: Identifying patterns and relationships
Strategy: Look for patterns
4. 45; 56   5. 144; 121
6. 72; 98; 128   7. 6,650; 9,850
8. 5,900; 6,650
Strategy: Logical reasoning
9. 1,000   10. 9,999
11. 1,001   12. 9,999
13. 1,000   14. 9,998
15. 1,003   16. 9,995
17. 1,023   18. 9,870

Chapter 2

Lesson 2.1

1. 1,034; 1,000 or 900
2. 10,985; 11,100 or 10,000
3. 269; 200 or 300   4. 17,975; 18,000
5. 846; 900 or 600   6. 595; 500
7. 752; 800 or 400   8. 19; 20
9. 49; 50   10. 29; 30
11.

Item	Actual Cost	Rounded to the Nearest Hundred
microwave	$450	$500
toaster	$80	$100
oven	$70	$100
coffee machine	$150	$200

The microwave is about $500 when rounded to the nearest hundred dollars.

The toaster is about $100 when rounded to the nearest hundred dollars.

The oven is about $100 when rounded to the nearest hundred dollars.

The coffee machine is about $200 when rounded to the nearest hundred dollars.

$500 + $100 + $100 + $200 = $900; Yes

Lesson 2.2

1. Yes   2. No   3. Yes   4. No
5. Yes   6. Yes   7. No   8. Yes
9. 1; 2; 3; 4; 6; 9; 12; 18; 36
10. 1; 2; 3; 4; 5; 6; 10; 12; 15; 20; 30; 60
11. 1; 2; 3; 4; 6; 12   12. 12
13. 1; 2; 3; 4; 6; 7; 12; 14; 21; 28; 42; 84
14. 1; 2; 3; 4; 6; 8; 9; 12; 18; 24; 36; 72
15. 1; 2; 3; 4; 6; 12   16. 12
17. 18; 24; 27; 30; 45   18. 18; 24; 30
19. 18; 24; 30   20. 19, 37, 47
21. 9, 15, 26, 33, 45
22. 11, 13, 17, 19, 23, 29
23. 21, 22, 24, 25, 26, 27, 28

Lesson 2.3

1. 40   2. 72   3. 72
4. 77   5. 70
6. 4; 8; 12; 16; 20; 24; 28; 32; 36; 40; 44; 48; 52; 56; 60; 64; 68; 72
7. 9; 18; 27; 36; 45; 54; 63; 72
8. 36; 72   9. 36
10. 6; 12; 18; 24; 30; 36; 42; 48
11. 8; 16; 24; 32; 40; 48; 56; 64
12. 24; 48   13. 24   14. 56
15. 36   16. 60   17. 60
18. 20; 48; 60; 72
19. 48; 72   20. 54; 72   21. 72

Put on Your Thinking Cap!

1. Thinking skill: Deduction
   Strategy: Make a systematic list, Guess and check
   The factors of 24 are 1, 2, 3, 4, 6, 8, 12, and 24.
   The number is 12.

2. Thinking skill: Deduction
   Strategy: Guess and check
   968

3. Thinking skill: Deduction
   Strategy: Make a systematic list

Now (Multiples of 4)	4	8	12	16	20	24
Next Year	5	9	13	17	21	25

Jane is 24 years old now.
More than one answer is possible.

4. Thinking skill: Analyzing
   Strategy: Guess and check

Number of Bicycles	Number of Tricycles	Total Number of Wheels
8	8	16 + 24 = 40
9	7	18 + 21 = 39
10	6	20 + 18 = 38

10 students are on bicycles.

5. Thinking skill: Deduction
   Strategy: Make a systematic list
   Multiples of 7: 7; 14; 21; 28; 35; 42; 49
   + 5: 12; 19; 26; 33; 40; 47; 54
   Multiples of 9: 9; 18; 27; 36; 45
   + 6: 15; 24; 33; 42; 51
   Michelle has 33 baseball cards.

Thinking skill: Logical reasoning
Strategy: Guess and check

6. 12 January   7. 17 January

8. Thinking skill: Sequencing
Strategy: Make a systematic list

Adventure Books ($4)	Soft Toys ($6)	Games ($8)
✓ ✓ ✓ ✓ ✓		
✓ ✓ ✓		✓
✓ ✓	✓ ✓	
✓		✓ ✓
	✓ ✓	✓

There are 5 different ways altogether.

Chapter 3

Lesson 3.1
1. 56; 5; 6   2. 5; 35; 3; 5
3. 6; 42; 4; 2   4. 2; 14; 1; 4
5.
```
        2, 6 5 8
    ×         7
    ------------
          5 6
        3 5 0
      4,2 0 0
    1 4,0 0 0
    ------------
    1 8,6 0 6
```
6. 3,960   7. 3,592   8. 8,343
9. 4,965   10. 10,767   11. 16,068
12. 21,693   13. 34,741   14. 43,976
15. 33,852

Lesson 3.2
1. 480   2. 890
3. 4; 92; 920   4. 3; 105; 1,050
5. 5; 2,095; 20,950   6. 2; 1,254; 12,540
7. 6; 3,216; 32,160   8. 6; 3,888; 38,880
9. 609; 6,090   10. 672; 6,720
11. 2,848; 28,480   12. 2,403; 24,030
13. 90; 40; 90 × 40 = 3,600

14. 400; 50; 400 × 50 = 20,000
15. 7,448   16. 5,238
17. 10,556   18. 24,288
19. 11,760   20. 31,608
21. 63,124   22. 80,464

Lesson 3.3
1.
```
       1                          1
   5)7 4 5                    5)7 4 5
     5 0 0                      5 0 0
                                2 4 5

     1 4                        1 4 9
   5)7 4 5                    5)7 4 5
     5 0 0                      5 0 0
     2 4 5                      2 4 5
     2 0 0                      2 0 0
       4 5                        4 5
                                  4 5
                                    0
```
2.
```
       1                          1
   6)9 8 4                    6)9 8 4
     6 0 0                      6 0 0
                                3 8 4

     1 6                        1 6 4
   6)9 8 4                    6)9 8 4
     6 0 0                      6 0 0
     3 8 4                      3 8 4
     3 6 0                      3 6 0
       2 4                        2 4
                                  2 4
                                    0
```
3. 364   4. 245   5. 237   6. 186
7. 109   8. 139   9. 123   10. 106

Lesson 3.4

1. 64; 8; 800
2. 63; 7; 700
3. 9; 3; 3000
4. 80; 20
5. 400; 80
6. 7,500; 1,500
7. 6,600; 1,100
8. 1,263
9. 1,013
10. 284
11. 562
12. 497
13. 968
14. 249 R 5
   1,748 is about 1,400.
   1,400 ÷ 7 = 200
   The answer 249 R 5 is reasonable.
15. 967 R 3
   3,871 is about 3,600.
   3,600 ÷ 4 = 900
   The answer 967 R 3 is reasonable.
16. 376 R 6
   3,014 is about 3,200.
   3,200 ÷ 8 = 400
   The answer 376 R 6 is reasonable.
17. 279 R 7
   2,518 is about 2,700.
   2,700 ÷ 9 = 300
   The answer 279 R 7 is reasonable.
18. 605 R 8
   5,453 is about 5,400.
   5,400 ÷ 9 = 600
   The answer 605 R 8 is reasonable.
19. 902 R 2
   7,218 is about 7,200.
   7,200 ÷ 8 = 900
   The answer 902 R 2 is reasonable.
20. 928 R 3
   6,499 is about 6,300.
   6,300 ÷ 7 = 900
   The answer 928 R 3 is reasonable.
21. 556 R 1
   2,781 is about 3,000.
   3,000 ÷ 5 = 600
   The answer 556 R 1 is reasonable.

Lesson 3.5

1. $699 × 38 = $26,562
   He collects $26,562.
2. 369 × 4 = 1,476
   1,476 blueberry muffins are sold every day.

3. 1,899 × 7 = 13,293
   It produces 13,293 toy cars in 7 days.
4. 3,438 ÷ 6 = 573
   Each group has 573 beads.
5. 2,255 ÷ 6 = 375 R 5
   a. Each post office receives 375 stamps.
   b. 5 stamps are left over.
6. a. $56 × 39 = $2,184
      A store has to pay $2,184.
   b. $72 × 39 = $2,808
      $2,808 − $2,184 = $624
      The store makes a profit of $624
      on the in-line skates.
7. $68 × 25 = $1,700
   $1,700 + $68 = $1,768
   Hannah and her mother gave $1,768 altogether
   to charity.
8. 2,400 − 15 = 2,385
   2,385 ÷ 9 = 265
   There are 265 oranges in each box.
9. 475 × 4 = 1,900
   1,900 + 475 = 2,375
   2,375 people are at the theater altogether.
10. 15 × 37 = 555
    555 − 20 = 535
    535 fish are put into the aquarium.
11. $3,650 − $1,610 = $2,040
    $2,040 ÷ 3 = $680
    Mr. Joseph puts $680 aside for each of his
    other expenses.
12. 1,543 + 932 = 2,475
    2,475 ÷ 9 = 275
    There is 275 milliliters of orange juice in each
    glass.

Put on Your Thinking Cap!

Thinking skill: Comparing
Strategy: Use a model

1. 275 × 3 = 825
   275 + 825 = 1,100
   1,100 − 156 = 944 beads
   There are 944 beads left.
2. 420 − 90 = 330
   420 + 330 = 750
   750 × 28 = 21,000
   The two factories produce 21,000 footballs
   in 28 days.

3.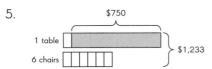

$392 ÷ 4 = $98
$98 × 3 = $294
$294 − $38 = $256
Sam has $256 now.

4. $89 × 6 = $534
$534 + $980 + $1,800 = $3,314
Mr. Roberts inherited $3,314.

5.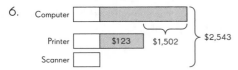

$1,233 − $750 = $483
$483 ÷ 7 = $69
$69 × 6 = $414
Mrs. Rodin pays $414 for the 6 chairs.

6.
Computer
Printer $123 $1,502 $2,543
Scanner

$1,502 + $123 = $1,625
The computer costs $1,625 more than the scanner.
$2,543 − $1,625 − $123 = $795
$795 ÷ 3 = $265
$265 + $1,625 = $1,890
Ms. Rao pays $1,890 for the computer.

7. Thinking skill: Logical reasoning
Strategy: Guess and check
a. Greatest possible product:
872 × 94 = 81,968
b. Least possible product:
489 × 27 = 13,203

8. Strategy: Make a systematic list

Multiples of 7	21	28	35	42	49	56	63
+ 3	24	31	38	45	52	59	66

45 is a multiple of 5.
Mr. Garcia is 42 years old now.
42 + 6 = 48
In 6 years, Mr. Garcia will be 48 years old.

9. Thinking skill: Analyzing parts and whole
Strategy: Restate the problem
2 bicycles have 4 wheels.
39 − 4 = 35 wheels for the same number
of bicycles and tricycles.

a. A bicycle and a tricycle have a total of
2 + 3 = 5 wheels
35 ÷ 5 = 7 tricycles
7 + 2 = 9 bicycles
The club buys 9 bicycles.
b. $49 × 9 = $441
The club pays $441 for the bicycles.

Chapter 4

Lesson 4.1

1. **Top Female Junior Sports Players**

Name	Basketball Points	Baseball Runs
Maria	88	59
Jade	110	64
Judith	121	60
Stacy	88	57

2. Jade; 64   3. Maria; Stacy

4. 7

5. **Living Things**

Snails	卌 ///
Worms	///
Ladybugs	卌 /
Butterflies	////

6. **Number of Living Things**

Snails	8
Worms	3
Ladybugs	6
Butterflies	4

7. 3   8. 10

9. worms; ladybugs

10. snails; butterflies or ladybugs; worms

11. **Bread Loaves Sold**

Whole grain bread	40
Raisin bread	55
Rye bread	30
Brown bread	40
White bread	65

12. 65   13. Whole grain; brown

14. White; whole grain; brown

15. Mystery books   16. Travel books

17. $80 + 30 + 20 + 50 + 60 = 240$

18. $60 + 80 = 140$ 19. $20 + 30 = 50$

20. $80 - 20 = 60$

Lesson 4.2

1. B; 5   2. E; 5

3. A; 4   4. D; 1

5. Check that the correct cell is shaded.

Grade	Soccer	Badminton	Base-ball	Basket-ball
2	6	10	**12**	12
3	6	9	8	**17**
4	**9**	7	14	10
5	7	**16**	6	11
Total	28	42	40	50

6. Basketball   7. Soccer

8. $17 - 11 = 6$ 9. 42 students

10. $50 - 42 = 8$ 11. The second grade

12. $40 - 28 = 12$

Lesson 4.3

1. June   2. March   3. April; May

4. Taylor's savings between January and June increased.

5. 9 A.M.   6. 12 P.M.

7. Between 9 A.M. and 11 A.M.;
   $390 - 240 = 150$ falafels

8. 50   9. 65

10. 7 A.M. and 8 A.M.   11. 3 hours

12. 55 patients   13. 70 patients

14. Between 3:30 P.M. and 4 P.M.; 25 patients

15. Between 6 P.M. and 7 P.M.; 25 patients

Put on Your Thinking Cap!

1. Bar graph. A bar graph is used to compare data using large numbers.

2. Line graph. A line graph is used to show how data changes over time.

3. Accept any correct answers.

1. D   2. B   3. B   4. C

5. C   6. C   7. D   8. C

9. C   10. A

11. sixty-seven thousand, ninety-eight

12. 15   13. 1,500   14. 27,000

15. 26,388; 27,888   16. $139

17. 54 ft   18. $240   19. 42   20. $69

21. a. 460 meters
    b. Between 2 and 3 minutes

22. 1 adult and 2 children;
    $$5 + $4 = 9
    $1,080 \div 9 = 120$
    120 adults are at the concert.

23. $2 + 11 = 13$ students
    Since 11 more grapes are needed to give the students exactly 7 grapes each, adding 2 and 11 will give the exact number of students.
    a. Ms. Ervine has 13 students.
       $13 \times 6 = 78$
       $78 + 2 = 80$
    b. There are 80 grapes in the basket.

Chapter 5

Lesson 5.1

1. $12 + 10 + 8 + 14 = 44$

2. $44 \div 4 = 11$ 3. 11

4. 26 in. $+ 28$ in. $+ 30$ in. $+ 32$ in. $+ 34$ in. $= 150$ in.

5. $150 \div 5 = 30$ in.   6. 30

7. 172   8. 700

9. 810   10. 79

11. Total age $= 15 + 12 + 16 + 17 = 60$
    Average age $= 60 \div 4 = 15$ years
    Alisha's age is the same as the average age.

12. Jose and Matthew   13. Daniel

14. $150 \times 3 = 450$ cm
    $145 \times 2 = 290$ cm
    $450 + 290 = 740$ cm
    $740 \div 5 = 148$ cm
    The mean height of the 5 students is 148 centimeters.

15. $1{,}896 \times 2 = 3{,}792$
$3{,}792 + 2{,}736 = 6{,}528$
$6{,}528 \div 3 = 2{,}176$
The average number of visitors is 2,176.

16. $136 \times 3 = 408$

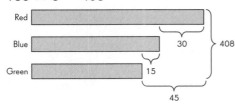

$408 - 45 - 15 = 348$
$348 \div 3 = 116$
There are 116 green beanbags in the store.

17. $264 \div 3 = 88$
$88 + 1 = 89$ (Science)
$89 + 5 = 94$ (Math)
$89 + 94 = 183$
$264 - 183 = 81$ (English)
Joleen's score in English is 81.

Lesson 5.2

1. 3, 4, 4, 5, 7, 9, 10
2. 5   3. 4
4. $10 - 3 = 7$
5. $\dfrac{3 + 4 + 4 + 5 + 7 + 9 + 10}{7} = \dfrac{42}{7} = 6$
6. 12 ft, 15 ft, 16 ft, 16 ft, 18 ft, 19 ft
7. 16 ft   8. 16 ft
9. $19 - 12 = 7$ ft
10. $\dfrac{12 + 15 + 16 + 16 + 18 + 19}{6}$
$= \dfrac{96}{6} = 16$ ft
11. 30 yd, 34 yd, 35 yd, 38 yd, 38 yd
12. 35 yd   13. 38 yd
14. $38 - 30 = 8$ yd
15. Mean $= \dfrac{30 + 34 + 35 + 38 + 38}{5}$
$= \dfrac{175}{5} = 35$ yd
16. $30 - 10 = 20$
17. 15   18. 20

19. $10 \times 1 = 10$
$15 \times 3 = 45$
$20 \times 2 = 40$
$25 \times 1 = 25$
$30 \times 2 = 60$
Total time $= 10 + 45 + 40 + 25 + 60$
$= 180$
Mean $= \dfrac{180}{9} = 20$

20. **Goals Scored**

Number of Goals	0	1	2	4	5	6
Number of Players	5	9	6	3	5	2

21. 30   22. 2   23. 1
24. $0 \times 5 = 0$
$1 \times 9 = 9$
$2 \times 6 = 12$
$4 \times 3 = 12$
$5 \times 5 = 25$
$6 \times 2 = 12$
$0 + 9 + 12 + 12 + 25 + 12 = 70$
25. 9   26. 24
27. 24   28. $25 - 20 = 5$
29. $20 \times 2 = 40$
$23 \times 2 = 46$
$24 \times 4 = 96$
$25 \times 1 = 25$
$40 + 46 + 96 + 25 = 207$
30. $207 \div 9 = 23$
31.

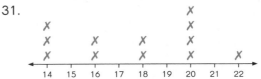

Foot Length (cm)

32. 12   33. 18
34. 20   35. 8
36.

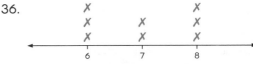

Number of Students on Each Bus

37. 7   38. 6 and 8
39. 2
40. Total number of students $= 18 + 14 + 24$
$= 56$
Mean $= 56 \div 8 = 7$

© Marshall Cavendish International (Singapore) Private Limited.

Lesson 5.3

1. 35   2. 30   3. 31
4. 59   5. 45
6. $\dfrac{34 + 42}{2} = \dfrac{76}{2} = 38$
7. $59 - 24 = 35$ 8. 59
9. Total height $= 24 + 30 + 33 + 34 + 42 + 45 + 45 + 59 = 312$
   Mean $= \dfrac{312}{8} = 39$
10. $275   11. $275
12. $309 - $205 = $104
13. $205
14. Total $= $205 + $264 + $268 + $275 + $275 + $276 + $284 + $292 + $309 = $2,448$
   Mean $= \dfrac{\$2,448}{9} = \$272$
15.

Number of Dogs Walked	
Stem	**Leaves**
1	0
2	5 5 6 7 8 8
3	2 3

$1 \mid 0 = 10$

16. 25; 28   17. 27
18. $33 - 10 = 23$
19. Total $= 10 + 25 + 25 + 26 + 27 + 28 + 28 + 32 + 33 = 234$
   Average $= \dfrac{234}{9} = 26$
20. 7

Lesson 5.4

1. less likely   2. certain
3. more likely   4. impossible
5. certain   6. Answers vary.
7. impossible   8. certain
9. equally likely   10. certain
11. 2   12. 6
13. 8   14. less likely
15. impossible   16. equally likely
17. impossible

Lesson 5.5

1. a. 2   b. 6   c. $\dfrac{2}{6} = \dfrac{1}{3}$
2. $\dfrac{1}{6}$ 3. $\dfrac{3}{6} = \dfrac{1}{2}$
4. $\dfrac{4}{6} = \dfrac{2}{3}$ 5. $\dfrac{6}{6} = 1$
6. $\dfrac{1}{10}$; less likely   7. $\dfrac{2}{10} = \dfrac{1}{5}$; less likely
8. $\dfrac{3}{10}$; less likely   9. $\dfrac{9}{10}$; more likely
10. $\dfrac{5}{12}$ 11. $\dfrac{6}{12} = \dfrac{1}{2}$
12. $\dfrac{9}{12} = \dfrac{3}{4}$ 13. $\dfrac{6}{12} = \dfrac{1}{2}$
14. $\dfrac{9}{12} = \dfrac{3}{4}$ 15. $\dfrac{3}{12} = \dfrac{1}{4}$
16.

(spinner: green, green, green, blue, red, purple, purple)

17. $\dfrac{2}{8} = \dfrac{1}{4}$
18. $\dfrac{4}{8} = \dfrac{1}{2}$ 19. $\dfrac{2}{8} = \dfrac{1}{4}$
20. $\dfrac{0}{8} = 0$

Lesson 5.6

1. $4 \times 16 = 64$
   $20 + 8 = 28$
   $64 - 28 = 36$
   Tony and Miguel scored 36 points altogether.
2. $196 - 88 = 108$
   $\dfrac{108}{2} = 54$
   The mean weight of the other 2 dolphins is 54 pounds.
3. $A + D + C = 52 \times 3 = 156$
   $A + D = 61 \times 2 = 122$
   $D + C = 44 \times 2 = 88$
   $C = 156 - 122 = 34$ snacks (Calvin)
   $D = 88 - 34 = 54$ snacks (Dakota)
   $A = 156 - 88 = 68$ snacks (Adrian)
4. $100 \times 76 - 100 \times 70 = 600$
   $600 \div (80 - 70) = 60$ (boys)
   $100 - 60 = 40$ (girls)
   40 girls took the quiz.

5. **Number of Letters**

Name	Number of Letters
Jessica	7
Brenda	6
Carl	4
Fiona	5
Jeremy	6
Barry	5
Nicole	6
Zoe	3
Ann	3

a.

Number of Letters

b. 6   c. $7 - 3 = 4$

d. Mean

$$= \frac{3 + 3 + 4 + 5 + 5 + 6 + 6 + 6 + 7}{9}$$

$$= \frac{45}{9} = 5$$

e. This will change the range and mean since there are 9 letters in *Annemarie*.
Only the mode will remain constant.

6. 87

7. $\frac{81 + 87}{2} = \frac{168}{2} = 84$

8. $98 - 46 = 52$

9. $\frac{46 + 54 + 63 + 81 + 87 + 87 + 92 + 98}{8}$

$$= \frac{608}{8} = 76$$

10. $76 \times 9 = 684$
$684 - 608 = 76$
The new player scores 76.

11. Total number of students = 20

The probability of a girl leaving $= \frac{3}{5} = \frac{12}{20}$
There are 12 girls.

12. a. Total number of crayons $= 3 + 2 + 4 + 3$
$= 12$

The probability of drawing a yellow crayon
$= \frac{4}{12} = \frac{1}{3}$

b. Number of red and green crayons
$= 3 + 3 = 6$
The probability of drawing a red or green
crayon $= \frac{6}{12} = \frac{1}{2}$

13. $\frac{\text{Number of buses}}{\text{Number of vehicles left}} = \frac{4}{19}$

14.

Math	Science

Total math and science score $= 74 \times 2 = 148$

Math	English

Total math and English score $= 83 \times 2 = 166$
$166 - 148 = 18$
She scored 18 more points in English than in science.

Put on Your Thinking Cap!

1. $147 \times 5 = 735$
$217 \times 2 = 434$
$735 + 434 = 1,169$
$1,169 \div 7 = 167$
He sells an average of 167 on newspapers on
each day of the week.

2. $78 \times 3 = 234$
$82 \times 4 = 328$
$328 - 234 = 94$
She will need to score 94 points to have
an average score of 82 points.

3. Thinking skill: Comparing
Strategy: Use a model

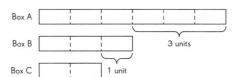

11 units ⟶ $88 \times 3 = 264$
1 unit ⟶ 24
$24 \times 6 = 144$
There are 144 paper clips in Box A.

4.

Mr. Clarkson [ ][$73]
Ms. Rose [ ][ ][ ][$38]

5 units ⟶ $\$180 \times 2 + \$38 - \$73 = \$325$
1 unit ⟶ $\$65$
$\$65 + \$73 = \$138$
$\$65 \times 4 - \$38 = \$222$
Mr. Clarkson had $138 and Ms. Rose had
$222 at first.

5. $68 \times 4 - 78 = 194$

Joyce, Mark, and Sarah have a total of 194 key chains.

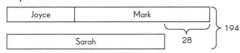

Sarah → $\dfrac{194 - 28}{2} = 83$

Joyce → $\dfrac{83 + 28}{3} = 37$

Mark → $37 \times 2 = 74$

Mark has 74 key chains.

6. With a difference of $(9 + 3) = 12$ points, the average score decreased by $(81 - 78) = 3$ points.

$12 \div 3 = 4$

There were 4 students in the group.

7. $145 \times 3 = 435$

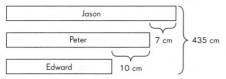

$435 - 17 - 10 = 408$

$408 \div 3 = 136$ cm (Edward's height)

$136 + 10 = 146$ cm (Peter's height)

$146 + 7 = 153$ cm (Jason's height)

Chapter 6

Lesson 6.1

1. $\dfrac{1}{9} + \dfrac{6}{9} = \dfrac{7}{9}; \dfrac{6}{9}; \dfrac{6}{9}$

2. $\dfrac{3}{6} + \dfrac{1}{6} = \dfrac{4}{6} = \dfrac{2}{3}; \dfrac{3}{6}; \dfrac{3}{6}$

3. $\dfrac{4}{10} + \dfrac{1}{10} = \dfrac{5}{10} = \dfrac{1}{2}$

4. $\dfrac{8}{12} + \dfrac{2}{12} = \dfrac{10}{12} = \dfrac{5}{6}$

5. $\dfrac{3}{12} + \dfrac{1}{12} = \dfrac{4}{12} = \dfrac{1}{3}$

6. $\dfrac{7}{12}$ 7. $\dfrac{1}{2}$ 8. $\dfrac{2}{3}$

9. $\dfrac{7}{8}$ 10. $\dfrac{7}{9}$

Lesson 6.2

1. $\dfrac{5}{6} - \dfrac{3}{6} = \dfrac{2}{6} = \dfrac{1}{3}; \dfrac{3}{6}; \dfrac{3}{6}$

2. $\dfrac{7}{12} - \dfrac{4}{12} = \dfrac{3}{12} = \dfrac{1}{4}; \dfrac{4}{12}; \dfrac{4}{12}$

3. $\dfrac{9}{12} - \dfrac{5}{12} = \dfrac{4}{12} = \dfrac{1}{3}$

4. $\dfrac{8}{10} - \dfrac{3}{10} = \dfrac{5}{10} = \dfrac{1}{2}$

5. $\dfrac{2}{12}; \dfrac{1}{6}$ 6. $\dfrac{2}{16}; \dfrac{1}{8}$

7. $\dfrac{1}{2}$ 8. $\dfrac{1}{12}$ 9. $\dfrac{1}{10}$ 10. $\dfrac{1}{8}$

Lesson 6.3

1. $1\dfrac{5}{6}$ 2. $3\dfrac{3}{8}$

3. $2\dfrac{4}{7}$ 4. $5\dfrac{7}{9}$

5. $2; 3; 2\dfrac{3}{4}$ 6. $4; 5; 4\dfrac{5}{6}$

7. $3; 2; 3\dfrac{2}{3}$ 8. $1\dfrac{3}{5}$ L

9. $2\dfrac{1}{4}$ lb   10. $2\dfrac{3}{5}$

11. $4\dfrac{5}{8}$ 12. $3\dfrac{4}{9}$

13. $5\dfrac{7}{12}$ 14. $2\dfrac{1}{6}$

15. $4\dfrac{3}{10}$ 16. $2\dfrac{3}{4}$

17. $1\dfrac{2}{5}$ 18. $4\dfrac{1}{3}$

19. $3\dfrac{3}{4}$ 20. $\dfrac{2}{5}; 1\dfrac{1}{5}; 1\dfrac{4}{5}; 2\dfrac{3}{5}$

21. $\dfrac{1}{2}; \dfrac{7}{8}; 1\dfrac{3}{4}; 2\dfrac{1}{8}; 2\dfrac{3}{4}$ 22. $4\dfrac{1}{2}; 6\dfrac{1}{4}; 7\dfrac{1}{2}$

23. $5\dfrac{1}{2}; 6\dfrac{2}{3}; 7\dfrac{1}{6}; 7\dfrac{5}{6}$

Lesson 6.4

1. a. 7   b. 3   c. 10   d. $\dfrac{10}{7}$

2. a. 16   b. 3   c. 19   d. $\dfrac{19}{8}$

3. a. 9   b. 2   c. 11   d. $\dfrac{11}{3}$

4. $\dfrac{8}{5}$ 5. $\dfrac{14}{3}$

6. $\dfrac{13}{2}$ 7. $2\dfrac{3}{5}; \dfrac{13}{5}$

8. $1\dfrac{5}{6}; \dfrac{11}{6}$ 9. $3\dfrac{7}{8}; \dfrac{31}{8}$

10. $5\dfrac{3}{4}; \dfrac{23}{4}$ 11. $2\dfrac{4}{9}; \dfrac{22}{9}$

12. $2\dfrac{1}{5}, \dfrac{11}{5}$ 13. $2\dfrac{3}{10}, \dfrac{23}{10}$

14. $3\frac{5}{8}$; $\frac{29}{8}$ 15. $\frac{7}{4}$; $\frac{9}{4}$; $\frac{11}{4}$

16. $\frac{5}{3}$; $\frac{7}{3}$; $\frac{8}{3}$ 17. $\frac{8}{7}$; $\frac{12}{7}$; $\frac{17}{7}$

18. $\frac{11}{3}$; $\frac{13}{3}$; $\frac{29}{6}$ 19. $\frac{9}{4}$; $\frac{11}{4}$; $\frac{15}{4}$

20. $\frac{21}{5}$; $\frac{26}{5}$; $\frac{29}{5}$ 21. $\frac{18}{5}$; $\frac{21}{5}$; $\frac{24}{5}$

22. $\frac{17}{15}$; $\frac{9}{5}$; $\frac{7}{3}$

Lesson 6.5

1. 1; 1   2. 2; 2

3. 12; 1; 1; 1   4. 20; 3; 3; 3

5. 20; 7; 2; 7; $2\frac{7}{10}$ 6. 21; 5; 3; 5; $3\frac{5}{7}$

7. 4; $2\frac{2}{3}$ 8. 4; $2\frac{1}{2}$

9. $7\frac{1}{2}$ 10. $1\frac{4}{5}$ 11. $2\frac{1}{3}$ 12. $1\frac{1}{4}$

13. $3\frac{1}{7}$ 14. 6   15. $7\frac{1}{2}$ 16. $8\frac{2}{5}$

17. $2\frac{2}{13}$ 18. $3\frac{1}{5}$ 19. 9; 11   20. 4; 5

21. 10; 13   22. 12; 17

23. 14; 4; 18   24. 18; 2; 20

25. $\frac{13}{3}$ 26. $\frac{23}{10}$ 27. $\frac{9}{7}$ 28. $\frac{14}{9}$

29. $\frac{9}{4}$ 30. $\frac{29}{12}$ 31. $\frac{13}{10}$ 32. $\frac{13}{11}$

33. $\frac{29}{5}$ 34. $\frac{35}{9}$ 35. $\frac{31}{5}$ 36. $\frac{51}{7}$

Lesson 6.6

1. $1\frac{2}{9}$ 2. $1\frac{2}{3}$ 3. $1\frac{3}{8}$ 4. $\frac{5}{6}$

5. $1\frac{1}{2}$ 6. $1\frac{1}{12}$ 7. $1\frac{5}{12}$ 8. $1\frac{1}{2}$

9. $1\frac{7}{12}$ 10. $1\frac{5}{8}$ 11. $2\frac{5}{12}$ 12. $3\frac{1}{9}$

13. $1\frac{1}{5}$ 14. $4\frac{1}{3}$ 15. $2\frac{1}{2}$ 16. $3\frac{1}{4}$

17. $5\frac{3}{10}$ 18. $2\frac{5}{14}$ 19. $1\frac{5}{12}$ 20. $4\frac{1}{9}$

Lesson 6.7

1. $\frac{2}{3}$ 2. $\frac{3}{5}$ 3. $\frac{1}{3}$ 4. $\frac{1}{3}$

5. 30, 6, 24, 24   6. 40   7. 25

8. 30   9. 16   10. 10   11. 12

Lesson 6.8

1. $90 - 40 - 20 = 30$

   $\frac{30}{90} = \frac{1}{3}$

   Arthur is left with $\frac{1}{3}$ of his money.

2. $1 - \frac{3}{4} = \frac{1}{4}$

   $\frac{1}{4} \times 20 = 5$

   The baker is left with 5 pounds of sugar.

3. a. $\frac{6}{10} = \frac{3}{5}$ of the fish are goldfish.

   b. Total number of fish $= 10 + 2 = 12$

   $\frac{4}{12} = \frac{1}{3}$ of the fish are angelfish.

4. $\frac{3}{10} + \frac{2}{5} = \frac{7}{10}$

   $\frac{7}{10}$ of her savings is spent.

5. $\frac{1}{2} + \frac{1}{8} = \frac{5}{8}$

   $1 - \frac{5}{8} = \frac{3}{8}$

   $\frac{3}{8}$ of the vehicles are neither cars nor motorcycles.

6. $6 + \frac{3}{10} = 6\frac{3}{10}$ meters

   Rajon's plant grows $6\frac{3}{10}$ meters high.

7. $\frac{2}{5}$ of $10 = 4$

   $\frac{1}{3} \times 4 = \frac{4}{3} = 1\frac{1}{3}$

   4 packets of turkey ham weigh $1\frac{1}{3}$ pounds.

8. $\frac{6}{4} \times 12 = 18$

   $\frac{1}{2} \times 18 = 9$

   Carla spends 9 hours lifting weights during the 12 days.

Put on Your Thinking Cap!

Thinking skill: Analyzing parts and whole

Strategy: Use a model

1.

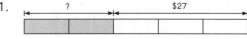

3 units → $27
1 unit → $27 ÷ 3 = $9
2 units → $9 × 2 = $18
Justin pays $18 for the shirt.

2.

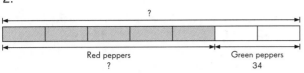

2 units ⟶ 34
1 unit ⟶ 34 ÷ 2 = 17
7 units ⟶ 17 × 7 = 119
The chef has 119 peppers altogether.

3.

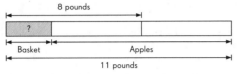

1 unit of apples ⟶ 11 − 8 = 3
8 − 3 = 5
The weight of the empty basket is 5 pounds.

4. Thinking skill: Analyzing parts and whole
Strategy: Guess and check

Answers vary.
One possible answer:

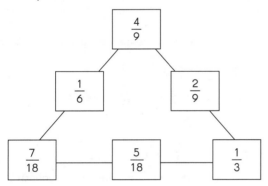

Mid-Year Test

1. C	2. D	3. B	4. C
5. B	6. B	7. C	8. D
9. D	10. A	11. B	12. D
13. B	14. C	15. B	16. A
17. D	18. C	19. B	20. C
21. 1		22. 371	
23. 10,283		24. 69; 138	
25. $\frac{1}{2}$		26. 27 cm; 156 cm	
27. $\frac{2}{3}$	28. 4 ft.	29. 19,256	
30. 66,150	31. 78	32. 1,549	

33. Saturday   34. 5,800
35. 900 − 800 = 100
36. 1$\frac{1}{6}$ liters   37. $\frac{4}{9}$
38. 3 units ⟶ 1,482
1 unit ⟶ 494
5 units ⟶ 494 × 5 = 2,470
There are 2,470 students in the school.
39. 200 + 100 = 300
Sakina and Alisha receive 300 tacos altogether.
40. $0.50 + $0.50 + $1 = $2
$36 ÷ $2 = 18
18 × 2 = 36
There are 36 50¢ coins in the bag.
41. 920 − 580 = 340
340 ÷ 2 = 170
170 plums are transferred from Basket A
to Basket B.
42. $3,328 ÷ 2 = $1,664

$1,664 ÷ 4 = $416
a. Each printer costs $416.
   $1,664 − $416 = $1,248
b. Each computer costs $1,248.
43. $\frac{8}{9}$ × 1,080 = 960

960 ÷ 10 = 96
96 × $2 = $192
Mr. Carlos collects $192 from the sale of apple.
44.

2 units ⟶ 76
1 unit ⟶ 76 ÷ 2 = 38
6 units ⟶ 38 × 6 = 228
They collected 228 seashells in all.
45. 45 − 9 = 36

$\frac{36}{3}$ × 4 = 48

48 − 8 = 40

$\frac{40}{2}$ × 3 = 60

60 passengers started the trip from the first
bus stop.